THE SIEGES OF
ALEXANDER
THE GREAT

THE SIEGES OF
ALEXANDER
THE GREAT

STEPHEN ENGLISH

Pen & Sword
MILITARY

First published in Great Britain in 2009 by
Pen & Sword Military
an imprint of
Pen & Sword Books Ltd
47 Church Street
Barnsley
South Yorkshire
S70 2AS

Copyright © Stephen English

ISBN 978 1 84884 060 7

A CIP catalogue record for this book is available from the British
Library.

Typeset in 11½pt Ehrhardt by
Pen & Sword Books Ltd., Barnsley

Printed and bound in Great Britain by
CPI Antony Rowe, Chippenham, Wiltshire

Pen & Sword Books Ltd incorporates the Imprints of
Pen & Sword Aviation, Pen & Sword Maritime, Pen & Sword Military,
Wharncliffe Local History, Pen and Sword Select,
Pen and Sword Military Classics and Leo Cooper.

For a complete list of Pen & Sword titles please contact
PEN & SWORD BOOKS LIMITED
47 Church Street, Barnsley, South Yorkshire, S70 2AS, England
E-mail: enquiries@pen-and-sword.co.uk
Website: www.pen-and-sword.co.uk

Contents

List of Plates

Preface

This book is the second of three dealing with the career of Alexander the Great. The first book, *The Army of Alexander the Great*, dealt with most issues pertaining to the army. Such issues will generally not be repeated in this volume or the next. The third volume is entitled *The Field Campaigns of Alexander the Great* and details every set-piece battle and minor campaign of Alexander's brief reign. These three volumes are each intended to stand alone, but are also complementary; when taken as a continuum, they detail every aspect of Alexander's military career.

The books arose out of my doctoral thesis and have, therefore, been six years in the preparation. I undertook the doctorate, and ultimately these books, with the intention of reconstructing Alexander's battles and sieges with a view to determining what tactics he used in gaining the largest empire the world had yet seen. This study, then, has a definite aim: to reconstruct Alexander's great battles and sieges and to assess tactics and their development throughout Alexander's career. This approach may be considered narrow and old-fashioned by some, but I believe much work remains to be done in the area, and that it is still a legitimate field of academic study.

I decided to undertake the thesis after having read Fuller a number of years ago; it constantly struck me that no real attempt has been made by academics to produce a more up-to-date assessment (Fuller was first published in 1958) based upon a considerable body of modern scholarship. Many articles have been written on individual battles and campaigns, but no full-length academic studies. I believe this full-scale approach has more validity, as an individual study will always, by necessity, miss the bigger picture and fail to grasp any developments in Alexander's tactical thinking. Small studies will also fail to properly demonstrate what Alexander's main tactics were, and if he used the same ideas repeatedly or constantly innovated to suit every circumstance.

The study of military history in recent years has become extremely unfashionable, and has been replaced by trendier subject areas like social history and the study of women in the ancient world (both very worthy fields of study in themselves, but not what interests me). This is extremely unfortunate, but I am sure that the pendulum will swing back in our direction at some point in the future. I have always been deeply fascinated by military history, and particularly the ancient world, for everything else depends upon warfare; upon victory and the freedoms it gave, or upon defeat and the travails it brought. As Sun Tzu said:

> The art of war is of vital importance to the state; it is a matter of life and death, a road to either victory or defeat. Hence it is a subject of inquiry which can on no account be neglected.[1]

I could not agree more.

One final note, all dates used within this work are BC, unless otherwise stated.

Acknowledgements

It is a great personal pleasure for me to now be able, with the help of my publisher and editor, to put some of my thoughts on paper, and hopefully pass on some of my interest to others who are of like mind. With this in mind, there are a number of people who deserve my thanks: firstly, Elizabeth for her continued love and support, my friends Martin and Sue Foulkes, and to my family. My greatest thanks, as always, are to Peter Rhodes for his boundless help and friendship. I would finally like to thank Phil Sidnell and the rest of the team at Pen and Sword for making this book possible.

Finally, I would say that this work owes a great debt to the many scholars who have come before me, and to the body of work that they have produced. I hope that in some small way I can add to that work. Despite the various people who have seen, read, and helped with the production of this book, any remaining errors are entirely my own.

Sources

The surviving source material for the career of Alexander the Great is usually divided into two general groups, the first of which is frequently referred to as the 'vulgate tradition' (or derivatives thereof). The term does far more harm to these sources than is probably justified: they present a popular tradition and are represented by Diodorus, Curtius, Pompeius Trogus (in the epitome of Justin) and Plutarch. It is not true to say that these sources are anti-Alexander, but they are certainly not as pro-Alexander as the other tradition, that represented by Arrian.

Diodorus

Of the five narratives that survive, Diodorus is the earliest. Diodorus Siculus was a Greek from Sicily, active in the first century BC, and author of a forty-book history that he called the *Library of History*. Of this great work, book seventeen deals with the career of Alexander. Diodorus is justly criticised by modern authorities for being an uncritical compiler of information. He also has a tendency to play with dates, to move events from one year to another in order to fill a time gap, and to even out events. Diodorus had a tendency to use a single primary source for each book, and in book seventeen this was Cleitarchus. He did, however, take information from other writers where appropriate, such as Ephorus, Apollodorus, Agatharchides and Timaeus. Some of his passages are almost identical to the corresponding passages in Curtius, taking into account differences in the Greek and Latin. The size of his work means that frequently he preserves some material that goes unrecorded in the other surviving sources and this is his primary value.

Diodorus' narratives are similar to the rest of the vulgate tradition, in that it is rhetorical in nature and contains, in the case of the Battle of the Hydaspes, for example, little of tactical interest. As in Plutarch, terminology, when used, is vague and lacking in full detail. For example, Porus divided his cavalry by posting a body on each flank and that he divided his elephants equally along the length of the front line.[2] The motif of the castle wall, with the elephants representing towers, is repeated throughout the vulgate tradition. Diodorus' descriptions of Alexander's dispositions are even less tactically useful, for example: 'he viewed those of the enemy and arranged his own forces accordingly.'[3] Diodorus also fails to recognize that there were several phases of the battle involving some intricate manoeuvres from Alexander.

Arrian

Lucius Flavius Arrianus (Arrian) was a Greek from Nicomedia in Bithynia (Asia Minor, modern Turkey). The specific date of his birth is nowhere attested, but since he was consul in 130 AD, he was most likely born some time around 85 AD. Although Arrian gained Roman citizenship, he was first and foremost a Greek, writing in Greek and primarily for a Greek audience. In his early life he was a pupil of the great Stoic philosopher, Epictetus, but his *Anabasis* (his history of Alexander) shows little or no bias in that direction. In his adult life, Arrian was a significant figure in the Roman Empire, along with the consulship he was also made governor of Cappadocia by Hadrian and commanded two Roman legions there. In terms of content, Arrian was no Thucydides, but he did choose good sources, even if his reason for the choice was dubious at best.[4]

Arrian's history has generally and rightly been regarded as the finest of the surviving narratives of the career of Alexander the Great. His text is unique in the ancient world in that he specifically gives us information about his use of sources: in his preface, he identifies both his sources and his reasons for using them as his primary sources. Arrian's reasons for selecting his sources are often considered naïve, and I believe this is a perfectly correct judgement, but we must examine his reasoning in more depth.

Arrian opens his history by telling us that:[5]

Wherever Ptolemy and Aristobulus in their histories of Alexander, the son of Philip, have given the same account, I have followed it on the assumption of its accuracy; where their facts differ I have chosen what I feel to be the more probable and interesting.

This statement may seem to imply that Ptolemy and Aristobulus were considered to be of equal weight by Arrian; this is demonstrably not the case, however. At 6.2.4 Arrian calls Ptolemy 'my principle source'; and for Arrian, therefore, there was evidently a clear hierarchy of quality with regard to his sources: Ptolemy, Aristobulus, and then the rest. Ptolemy is clearly Arrian's main narrative source, and some passages are probably verbatim extracts, such as the narrative of the Danubian campaign. Whilst we can clearly see Ptolemy in the text of Arrian, Aristobulus' contribution is more difficult to assess. The surviving fragments of Aristobulus, coupled with the relative lack of direct citations in Arrian, means that there is insufficient primary material to make any substantive judgements.

Bias is always present in any written material, and in history particularly so. The surviving sources for the career of Alexander are especially prone to this, given that what we have was written so long after his death, and the now-lost contemporary sources were written by individuals who can certainly be accused of having ulterior motives. Ptolemy, for example, has been accused of deliberately altering events to make Perdiccas responsible for the destruction of Thebes.[6] Perdiccas and Ptolemy were rivals in the period immediately after Alexander's death; Perdiccas having invaded Ptolemy's Egypt in 320. If Ptolemy wrote his history around this time, then there was an obvious and strong political motivation for wishing to re-write history in his favour and against Perdiccas. None of the dates for Ptolemy's history are anywhere near this early, however, so we must look more deeply for Ptolemy's motives. It is almost certainly incorrect to assume simple political bias, however. Ptolemy explicitly tells us that Perdiccas was wounded in the initial stages of combat, and was removed from the field, taking no further part in the battle. Any bias in Ptolemy's account is not anti-Perdiccas but is in fact pro-Alexander. Ptolemy has Alexander giving the Thebans every chance to surrender and essentially blames them for their fate. I see no reason, therefore, to dismiss Arrian's account on the grounds of bias against one of his later protagonists.

The Perdiccas bias, or lack thereof, is further complicated by a very similar incident during the siege of Halicarnassus. Arrian tells us that two drunken solders from Perdiccas' *taxis* (division of heavy infantry) made some kind of approach to the city, and were killed by missile fire from the defenders, some of whom began shooting at the rest of the encamped Macedonians. Perdiccas ordered more troops to join the fray, as did Memnon, and considerable confusion ensued. Arrian tells us that Alexander could have broken into the city at this point but sounded the withdrawal. The Diodorus version of events is considerably briefer, and whilst Arrian represents it as an almost total success, with the city coming close to falling, Diodorus has it as an unqualified defeat.[7] Again, this incident does not show a bias against Perdiccas because, although he clearly acted without orders, the city could have fallen because of his actions and was only prevented from doing so by Alexander. If Ptolemy was genuinely anti-Perdiccas, then we can only assume that he would have taken the same line as Diodorus and presented the incident as a disaster.

The sources are also far from comprehensive in terms of what was written; with regard to the siege of Tyre, it is certain that the texts of Arrian and Curtius omit much of the detail of the siege. There is certainly not enough narrative to fill the eight months that we know it took Alexander to capture the island fortress. One obvious and significant omission is the construction of the mole; it seems to disappear from Arrian and Curtius for quite some time. One minute it is being destroyed by the fire ship, the next it has been doubled in size and is at the very walls of Tyre itself.[8] Diodorus provides a little vital tactical information, that after early mistakes Alexander was protecting the construction workers with a heavy screen of naval vessels. The main reason could be that Ptolemy may have only included the most interesting elements of the siege, which is entirely plausible; but it is also possible that Ptolemy may not have been present for parts of the siege.[9] Junior officers would likely have been sent, from time to time, on scouting or foraging missions. The lack of Ptolemy's name in the histories at this point makes it impossible to know. Arrians' choice of a junior officer (Ptolemy) in the army for the first few years of the campaign, a man who may have been excluded from councils of war during that time, adds yet another layer of complexity to the interpretation of his text.

Curtius

Quintus Curtius Rufus wrote in the second quarter of the first century AD. He was a Roman, writing in Latin, and was himself an active politician, having held public offices under both Tiberius and Claudius. Curtius wrote his history of Alexander in ten books, of which the first two are now lost, and what remains contains lacunae in places (the end of book five and the beginning of book six, and large parts of book ten, for example). Curtius' primary source seems to have been Cleitarchus, but he sensibly added many details from Ptolemy and others.

Although Arrian is correctly regarded as the most reliable of the surviving sources, there is much in Curtius and others that is not in Arrian; either because the latter did not believe it important, or perhaps because he did not have access to the material. At Issus, for example, Curtius presents us with a picture of events at the Persian court that is not in Arrian. He describes a debate, not with Amyntas as in Arrian, but with Thymondas, son of Mentor.[10] The subject of the debate, according to Curtius, was whether or not to divide the army, a theme that appears in neither Arrian nor Plutarch. Curtius and Diodorus both describe an earlier debate in Babylon, in which the Athenian mercenary, Charidemus, advocated such a division of forces, and was executed for his overzealousness. This should not necessarily be taken to imply that Curtius had access to a Persian source that Arrian did not, perhaps only that Curtius was occasionally interested in issues outside of Arrian's scope.[11]

Curtius' narrative is replete with rhetoric and anecdotal material, as with the other vulgate sources. Curtius does, however, present us with valuable topographical information that is so often missing from Arrian, such as the width of the Hydaspes River, the islands in the river, the island upon which Alexander mistakenly landed, the slippery ground after the rains and the plain where the final battle occurred.[12] Curtius tends to pay little attention to tactical movements, and more to individual *aristeia* (courage, bravery etc.), and is therefore of lesser use in a tactical study than Arrian, but still can not be ignored.

Curtius is not primarily interested in the characters of the various protagonists in the way that Plutarch is, but on occasion his narrative does tend in this direction (too much for our purposes at least). At Gaugamela, for example, Curtius' objective is to highlight the activities of the principal characters, Alexander, Darius and Parmenio, the latter of whom he accuses of gross dereliction of duty, and not to provide a coherent narrative of events. His account of this particular battle is, therefore, problematic to say the least.

All of our sources like to present Alexander as the Homeric hero, but perhaps Curtius is more guilty of it than others. The story found in Curtius (although interestingly not Arrian) of Batis being dragged around the circuit of the city behind Alexander's chariot is an intriguing one.[13] The Homeric story presents Achilles dragging Hector's *corpse* behind his chariot, but here Batis is still alive.

Curtius does, occasionally, give us a useful insight into Alexander's thinking by means of a discussion of character. During the siege of Tyre, for example, Curtius presents us with a picture of a depressed Alexander, a man undecided whether to continue with the siege, or to abandon it; his decision to stay, coming only with the arrival of the Cypriot fleet.[14] This is almost certainly another instance of Curtius misunderstanding his sources. It is likely that Alexander considered leaving to campaign elsewhere as he did at Halicarnassus, but not that he considered abandoning the siege altogether as Curtius suggests.

Arrian is usually the source that looks to remove or reduce blame from Alexander in the event of things not going according to plan, but on occasion Curtius is just as apologetic. During the siege of Tyre, for example, Curtius places the expedition against the Arabs before the assault by the fire ship. This seems an obvious device to remove any blame from Alexander by having him away from the siege on expedition in the Lebanese Mountains at the time of this disastrous counter-attack by the Tyrians, only to have him return, restore order and redouble efforts to construct the mole, this time with proper defences in place.

The general picture presented here of Arrian providing technical details, whilst the vulgate focuses on personalities, is far from universally true. At Tyre, for example, Arrian's account lacks depth and tends to focus on personalities rather than technical detail, and although it does provide us with a reasonable chronology of events, the account is brief and much must have been missed or omitted; that is to say nothing of evident errors discussed earlier. Curtius' account on the other hand is shorter, but contains a greater amount of technical information. On this occasion, Curtius' source is evidently the superior one, probably Cleitarchus. Curtius' narrative shows enough similarities with Arrian and Diodorus for us to conclude that Cleitarchus was not Curtius' only source. Much of the technical detail in Curtius' narrative must have been provided by a technically proficient eye witness.

Elsewhere in his work, Curtius cites three sources: Cleitarchus, Timagenes and Ptolemy.[15] Neither Cleitarchus nor Timagenes are likely to have been the primary source for any battle narrative (although Cleitarchus can probably be considered to be Curtius' primary source overall), and an examination of commonalities with Arrian, who is undoubtedly based upon Ptolemy, shows that he was not Curtius' main source either; although there are enough commonalities to suggest that he did indeed have access to Ptolemy's account. Curtius' attitude towards Parmenio provides us with some clues as to his main source; in places he follows a tradition that is favourable towards Parmenio, whilst being hostile towards Menidas, who was heavily implicated in Parmenio's murder, although there is undoubted criticism of Parmenio also.[16]

Curtius' picture of Alexander himself is also rather different from that which would have been found in Callisthenes. Alexander is depicted as gnashing his teeth in frustration and rage at the escape of Darius, but Curtius perhaps goes too far in describing Alexander as indecisive and prone to panic. This presentation of Alexander tallies nicely with the often-positive picture presented of Parmenio, as noted above. Curtius links his occasionally-negative picture of

Alexander with an improbable description of the whole Macedonian army as also being prone to panic.

Plutarch

Plutarch was a famous biographer who wrote a series of parallel 'lives' of famous Greeks and Romans, every Greek being paired with a Roman counterpart; Alexander being paired with Julius Caesar. All of Plutarch's lives survive, bar two: Epaminondas and Scipio. Plutarch wrote towards the end of the first century and the beginning of the second century AD, although the exact dates of his life are not known with certainty. He was a Greek, originally from Chaeronea, but, like Arrian, he had also been granted Roman citizenship. The primary problem with Plutarch is that he was writing biography and not history: he usually favours stories that illustrated some character trait in his subject, even if the historicity of the event was dubious, such as the taming of Bucephalus episode.

Plutarch's stated aim, to write biography and not history, shows a fine appreciation of the differences between the two. He should not be criticised too strongly by historians for failing to provide a great deal of information that is useful in reconstructing narrative, as this was not his purpose. The lack of useful information in Plutarch is even more acute for the military historian, as he shows almost no appreciation for tactical terminology and its use. He does, however, sometimes refer to sources that others do not. At the Hydaspes, for example, Plutarch's account of the battle is based almost entirely on 'Alexander's letters',[17] although other sources are cited. These include Onesicritus and Sotion, as well as 'most writers' when he clearly does not wish to divulge his source specifically. Given his lack of interest in strategy and tactics, he is of little use to military narratives except in occasional points of detail, or references to non–standard sources such as the 'letters'.

Pompeius Trogus

Much like Diodorus, Pompeius Trogus wrote a world history, but unlike Diodorus, little survives. Trogus was a romanized Gaul originally from Vasio and, like the rest of the vulgate, used Cleitarchus heavily, although he also relied upon Timagenes. One of the main reasons that Trogus does not survive is the success of the much-abbreviated, and evidently of far poorer quality, epitome of

Justin. Historians typically refer to this source as being 'Justin' rather than 'Pompeius Trogus' specifically because of that success, and I have followed that tradition throughout this work.

Attitudes to Parmenio

Some of the key differences in our surviving sources, and indeed in the primary sources that they relied upon can be found in the attitudes to the elder statesman Parmenio. He is sometimes presented as the wise old general acting as a foil to the youthful exuberance of Alexander, but more often, particularly by Arrian, as being overly cautious and lacking the same heroic vision of the king.

There are five instances in Arrian where Alexander considers (however briefly) and then rejects the advice of Parmenio.[18] The first of which is a dialogue that occurred at the Granicus. What ensued is only reported in Arrian and Plutarch; a debate between Alexander and Parmenio as to the best course of action. Parmenio apparently advised waiting until the morning. He believed the Persians, who were greatly inferior in infantry, would withdraw and the Macedonians could get across the river unopposed early the following day. He also, apparently, emphasized the difficulties of the terrain. Both sources have Parmenio's advice being rejected out of hand by Alexander with very little serious consideration.

This is part of a much-used, and often discussed, device of (particularly) Arrian to have the overly-cautious Parmenio's advice rejected by the bold and heroic Alexander. Diodorus has no such debate, but his account of the battle is as if the advice were acted upon. We must note that Ptolemy was fighting in roughly the same area as Alexander, the right wing, and so Ptolemy was probably also glorifying his own role in the battle as well as that of the king, and not simply criticizing the overly-cautious Parmenio. He may also simply have had less knowledge of events on the left, and chosen to concentrate on events that he was directly involved in. At the Granicus, Callisthenes was Arrian's source for at least the debate with Parmenio. Callisthenes is known to have been hostile to Parmenio and is probably the source for all five of the dialogues between Alexander and the old general that show him as being too cautious and set him against Alexander's youthful heroism.

Before the siege of Halicarnassus began in earnest, we have another debate between Parmenio and Alexander as to the wisdom of offering a naval battle. This is significantly different from the other such debates: here Alexander is portrayed as the pragmatic and cautious party, in opposition to Parmenio's rash and impetuous suggestion. It is perhaps unwise to pass judgment on Parmenio at this point, as we have no indication as to exactly what plan he proposed, although it would probably have been more sophisticated than a simple battle between all available forces.

At Gaugamela, Parmenio is treated favourably by Diodorus, a fact which presents a number of problems. This treatment decreases the likelihood that he was influenced by the negative sentiment in Callisthenes. It could be argued that the prominent place of the Thessalian cavalry in both Diodorus and Plutarch suggests a commonality of source; but I think it more likely that, in the absence of specific passages that are obviously from the same source, their prominent role in both is simply a reflection of actual events. That is to say that they in fact did have a significant role in the battle, and Diodorus and Plutarch are simply honestly reflecting this.

The incident of the call for help by Parmenio at the Battle of Gaugamela, just after Alexander had begun the pursuit of Darius, is also interesting. Again, it shows no malice towards Parmenio at all by Arrian or his source, but simply presents a picture of the Thessalians in genuine difficulty asking for help. Diodorus, in common with Arrian, simply presents Alexander's response without comment, unlike Plutarch and Curtius who note Alexander's frustration at the request. Interestingly, along with Diodorus' attributing no blame to Parmenio for this incident, he also attributes no blame to Alexander. Diodorus' account of this particular battle is far less useful than Curtius or Arrian, but should not be ignored as it provides some corroboration of other sources in some key details.

On a final note, I have tried to avoid being dogmatic in my approach to the sources; it is certainly true that Arrian seems to be the most reliable of the surviving material, but I have not used him to the exclusion of any of the other sources, including non-literary material where appropriate. The vulgate tradition can offer much that is of interest to the military historian, and where they disagree with Arrian it is a mistake to always assume that they are incorrect.

Chapter 1

Siege technology

For much of early Greek history the defenders in any siege situation almost invariably had the upper hand. Walls were generally fairly strong and the only real mechanisms that an attacking army had available were ladders, primitive rams, occasionally sapping (although, surprisingly, this does not seem to have been too common), betrayal and starvation. During a siege where scaling ladders were, effectively, the major means of attack, it is not surprising that most sieges were unsatisfactory, at least from the perspective of the attacking force. Frequently sieges turned out to be lengthy affairs and were won and lost by attrition or betrayal. Successful diplomacy was vital during the classical and archaic periods for a besieger to achieve success, and was raised to a virtual art form by Philip. Philip II, the father of Alexander the Great, was once quoted as saying that he could capture any city as long as he could get a mule laden with gold to the gates. This is a strong indication of the power of bribery and betrayal as a tool for a successful besieger. This situation changed radically with the invention of an entirely new weapon of war: the catapult.

Catapults

The catapult, as we would understand it, is one of those technological advances that have a clear and precise date and location for its invention. It was invented in Syracuse under the auspices of Dionysius I in, or very near to, 399. Earlier references have sometimes been argued, but are not convincing.[19] Diodorus is the first historian to describe the new invention in detail; he tells us in that year 'the entire city became one great arsenal'.[20] It seems that Dionysius gathered from all over Sicily the finest engineers of the day to construct for him vast quantities of the most modern pieces of military technology. As well as manufacturing current pieces of technology, these engineers and artisans were almost certainly also to undertake research and development work into other entirely new forms of armaments. From this research work the catapult was first developed. Diodorus goes on to tell us that[21]:

> He (Dionysius I) gathered skilled workmen, commandeering them from the cities under his control, and attracting them by high wages from Italy and Greece, as well as Carthaginian territory. For his purpose was to make weapons in great numbers and every kind of missile, and also quadriremes and quinquiremes... not only was every space, such as the porticoes and back rooms of the temples as well as the gymnasia and colonnades of the market place crowded with workers, but the making of great quantities of arms went on. In fact the catapult was invented at this time in Syracuse... a natural consequence of the assembly in one place of the most skilful craftsmen from all over the world.

The first catapult, called the *gastraphetes*, or belly-bow, was a simple device. It was essentially a bow, although it was larger than that which a man could draw using his strength alone. A ratchet mechanism was added to allow the draw string to be drawn further back, and to keep it in position longer than could be achieved by a man holding a bow string in position. To load the weapon, one end was braced against the stomach of the user (hence the name), and the other against the ground or a wall. Both hands were then used to draw back the bow string and hook it to one of the teeth of the ratchet where it sat awaiting the weapon being fired. This early artillery was, essentially, little more than a large crossbow, although it should not be easily dismissed as it was from this weapon that the later ballistae were developed. The bow section of the *gastraphetes* was also slightly different from regular design, as it had to withstand greater stresses than a normal bow. In order to achieve this, the bow was constructed of a compound design. A compound bow would have been made up of three distinct layers. The core of the bow would have been wood, as with a regular weapon. On the inside (the side facing the operator) was glued a layer of horn, providing considerable strength, far greater than a simple wooden bow would have been capable of. On the outside of the device (the side facing the enemy) was glued a layer of sinew. These two diverse materials were both vital to the operation of the bow. The horn essentially resisted compression, and the sinew resisted stretching, and both snapped back into their rest position with considerable force when the tension on them was released. The result of this was that the bow would be under considerable stress when drawn back and ready for firing, and would always seek to return to the rest position.[22] The tactical uses of the *gastraphetes* were limited, as the arrow was placed loose in a groove at the front of the device and, therefore, the *gastraphetes* could only be aimed horizontally or upwards. The weapon could not be aimed downwards because the arrow was likely to slide out of the groove. The *gastraphetes*, therefore, was of no use in defending a fortification when the operator would be on a wall or in a defensive tower; it was only of use in assaulting a fortified position.

Early catapults spread from Sicily to Greece at an unknown date in the fourth century. It is far from clear how quickly these new non-torsion catapults spread to the mainland, or how widespread they became at an early date. A significant turning point certainly occurred in 354 when Philip was first beginning to become involved in the affairs of Thessaly. He met, and was quickly defeated by, Onomarchus of Phocis. The latter achieved this success by the use of a quite brilliant stratagem. Onomarchus lured the Macedonians into a horseshoe-shaped canyon where they could use catapults stationed out of reach on the cliff tops of the canyon walls. It seems unlikely that the Macedonians possessed artillery before this point because this incident had a significant impact on Philip, prompting him to instruct his engineers to construct siege engines, and no doubt to conduct research into better and more powerful designs. Developments in Macedonia were apparently slow, as the Macedonian siege train had had little impact anywhere until the siege of Perinthus in 340, some fourteen years later. Even by this time Diodorus only records arrow-shooting catapults as being in the possession of Philip; Arrian adds to this the key point that 'Macedonian stone-throwers do not appear until Alexander's attack on Halicarnassus some years later'.[23]

Macedonian engineers were apparently slow to develop the new technology, and perhaps Philip's patronage was rather less generous than we may otherwise have presumed. It would appear, however, that this slow pace of development was echoed throughout the Greek world. There appears to have been a fairly considerable delay between the invention of the *gastraphetes* and the discovery of the principle of torsion; this is essentially where the propulsive force is provided by the twisting of some material, such as sinew, hair or rope, rather than a bow (which can be described as a non-torsion engine). The first torsion catapult was probably similar in some ways to the *gastraphetes*. Its overall design was similar, the string was drawn back, this time by the use of a mechanical mechanism rather than manpower, its overall appearance was similar to a crossbow, but instead of a bow at the front it had two arms. In essence it looked as though the bow had been cut in two at the centre, with the centre point of each half anchored on to a frame. This new design also incorporated a certain amount of extra wood in the framework of the device to cope with the extra stress that the machine would be subject to, especially at the front end where the two struts were attached to the frame. This device was capable of firing either an arrow or a small shot over a much greater distance than the simple non-torsion compound bow.

Macedonian engineers evidently had been investigating the three materials that constituted the compound bow of the *gastraphetes*, namely sinew, wood and horn, and had come to the belief that, of the three, the sinew was the material that provided by far the greatest propulsive force. The principle of torsion came out of their desire to isolate and magnify this force in order to fire larger arrows or shot, and to do it over greater distances than achievable by a normal compound bow.

The torsion principle was probably discovered, or at least developed into the standard two-arm device described above, in Macedonian at some point during the mid fourth century. The date is conventionally thought to be around 340 under the auspices of Philip II, although the first positive evidence for torsion springs date from between 338-326, during the reign of Alexander.[24] We do know, however, that Alexander used stone-throwing catapults against Halicarnassus and probably Miletus in 334, and they would certainly have been torsion engines in order to provide the propulsive force necessary to do any damage at all to the walls. Given this, I believe the discovery of the principle of torsion can be narrowed down further to between 340-334; more than this cannot be claimed with any degree of certainty.

Alexander's stone-throwing catapults were of a rather different design than the 'crossbow' type of device, like the *gastraphetes*. Alexander's single-armed stone-throwing catapults, called a *mongakon*, would have been similar in design, although perhaps less powerful, than the better known, but rather later, Roman *onager*. This was essentially a more traditional catapult design. Ammianus, a later Roman historian, described the Roman *onager* as follows:[25]

The *onager's* framework is made out of two beams from oak, which curve into humps. In the middle they have quite large holes in them, in which strong sinew ropes are stretched and twisted. A long arm is then inserted between the bundle of rope, at its end it has a pin and a pouch. It strikes on a huge buffer with a sack stuffed with fine chaff and secured by tight binding. When it comes to combat, a round stone (often clay balls with Greek fire in them, which explode on impact and burst into flames) is put in the pouch and the arm is winched down. Then, the master artilleryman strikes the pin with a hammer, and with a big blow, the stone is launched towards its target.

The description is useful, as Alexander's device would have been of similar design and operation, although, as noted above, would have been rather less advanced. The *mongakon* was essentially a mechanized staff sling; it consisted of a long shaft with a slingshot pouch at the end that was projected forwards by means of tension built up in rope at the fixed end of the staff.

Alexander's stone throwing devices represent a major shift in the balance of power during the conduct of siege operations. For the first time a besieging army could directly assault a city's walls with a weapon far more powerful and devastating than a large arrow. The attackers now had the very real possibility of punching a hole through the defences of a besieged fortress, or of bringing down stretches of walls from a distance with the defenders being able to do very little about it other than hastily constructing a second layer of walls behind the section under attack, as the defenders did at Halicarnassus in 334. From this point forwards, the besieger would have the very real possibility of capturing any fortified position by force, rather than by attrition or deception. Alexander was to use this tactical shift brilliantly throughout his career. It was partly this development, and the success it helped Alexander achieve, that prompted Lane Fox to note that 'it was as a stormer of cities that [Alexander] left his most vigorous impression'.[26] Alexander may have been more famous as a field commander, but I hope to demonstrate during this book that he was a truly brilliant besieger of cities.

Catapults were the terror weapons of their day; there is little doubt that they would have spread fear amongst those who were on the receiving end. To this end, they were not just used in sieges, but during field campaigns too, as demonstrated on two occasions during Alexander's career. They did not have to be particularly effective against the opposition in terms of casualties to have a profound impact on their morale. In all of the many field campaigns that Alexander conducted, there are only two instances where he deployed artillery pieces against troops deployed in the open; both of which demonstrate very clearly their impact on the battlefield.

The first incident occurred after Alexander had been compelled to temporarily abandon the siege of Pellium in 335, and was in the process of extricating his troops from the trap in which he had found himself, to a safer area beyond the Eordaicus River. Most of his troops managed to cross safely and gathered on the other side, but his rearguard, consisting of the Agrianians and some archers, had considerable difficulty in disengaging from the enemy that were pressing them hard. Arrian describes the situation:[27]

> He deployed his artillery on the bank of the river and ordered his men to shoot, at maximum range, all the types of missile that are hurled from machines. He also ordered the archers, who had already plunged in, to shoot from mid-stream. Glaucias' men did not dare to advance within range. Meanwhile the Macedonians crossed the river safely, so that not one casualty was suffered in the withdrawal.

Glaucias' men did not dare advance within range of the catapult bolts, even though none of them were actually killed during the opening volley when they were in range. This psychological impact was clearly devastating and achieved exactly Alexander's desired result of being able to disengage his troops and safely allow them to cross the river without being harried by the natives. This effect was almost certainly partly due to the catapult being a new form of weapon; it is highly likely that this was the first time the weapons had been seen by any of the inhabitants of that area of the Balkans.

The second incident of Alexander's employment of catapults during field operations also occurred in the context of a river crossing, this time offensively rather than to cover a withdrawal. At the crossing of the Jaxartes River in 329, a group of Scythians was occupying the far bank, making any attempt at crossing extremely hazardous, as the Macedonians would have been at a severe disadvantage against these excellent horsemen and horse archers. Arrian records the events that followed:[28]

> When all the skin floats were ready and the army in full equipment drawn up on the river bank, the catapults, at the word of command, opened up on the Scythians who were riding along the edge of the water on the further side. Some of them were hit; one was pierced through both shield and breastplate and fell dead from his horse. The Scythians were taken completely aback by the long range of the catapults, and that, together with the loss of a good man, induced them to withdraw a short distance from the river, whereupon Alexander, seeing their consternation, ordered the trumpets to sound and himself led the way over the water, followed by his men.

Again, we can see that the actual impact of the catapult in a field operation was minimal, only one Scythian was killed, but the psychological impact of these weapons of apparently-limited destructive capability (outside of siege operations that is) was far greater than their operational effectiveness would warrant.

These two examples (along with the Onomarchus incident) of the use of artillery in the field illustrate very well the limited theatre in which they could be employed effectively, but also the devastating impact that they could have, especially when employed against enemies who had not seen these weapons before. They had to be close enough to the enemy in order for their projectiles to reach; they also had to be on ground that was easily defensible, or did not require defending at all. These examples show very clearly the psychological effect of these weapons was out of all proportion to their actual physical effectiveness. On the two occasions when Alexander employed catapults in the field, only one man is recorded as being killed, and yet they helped in ensuring a successful outcome to both operations. Their true usefulness in field operations lay in their shock value, and in the confusion that they caused amongst the enemy, although this was exacerbated by the fact that on each occasion the enemy had never before seen such weapons. We can not be sure how effective they would be if used again, or against a more experienced or better prepared opponent. We can probably also argue that warriors such as the Scythians may well have been prepared to die in hand-to-hand combat; but they were evidently not so prepared to risk their lives when there was no possibility of striking back at the enemy.

Catapults of the *gastraphetes* type were small, hand-held devices and could be easily transported from one siege to another. Once the principle of torsion was developed and catapults took on a rather larger structure, this became more problematic. They could no longer be carried by an individual and would have to be transported (and perhaps disassembled first) by cart or mule from place to place. The result of this was that they were likely to be designed to be dismantled while not in operation. This was partly for ease of transport and partly to ensure that the sinew was only under stress when the machine was in operation. This would prevent any reduction in the propulsive force provided by the sinew over time. The catapults, then, were in all likelihood 'flat-packed' for transportation over any distance and this is why we frequently hear of Alexander arriving at a city and having to wait for a period of time for the siege engines to catch up. This occurred at Tyre, Gaza and every siege after 332 in the northeast of the former Persian Empire, as well as in India. It would seem impossible for a fully-constructed catapult, or any of Alexander's other siege engines (towers and rams, for example), to have been easily transported across desert, rivers or mountains like the Hindu Kush without first being dismantled. Scaling ladders could easily be built on site as a siege was about to begin, but better quality examples were probably also transported with the rest of the siege train. The ladders that collapsed at the city of the Mallians were probably hastily constructed and of rather poor quality.

We hear frequently of Alexander's famous siege train; for most of his career he required his army, or more likely flying columns detached from the main army, to move at considerably greater speeds than a mule and cart was capable of. This led, at almost every siege, to his arriving before his siege engines, which had to be brought up later. At Gaza, for example, there is a delay of several days as the engines were brought first by ship, and then dragged across the desert, from Tyre. Again, throughout the Indian campaign we see a similar situation where Alexander is usually delayed by a week or more waiting for his engines so he could begin the siege proper. In India this time was usually spent fortifying his camp and by constructing a double stockade around the fortification that he was besieging. This kind of circumvallation is not particularly common in Greek warfare, but became so during the Roman period, Julius Caesar being a particularly fine exponent of their use. See for example, his campaigns in Gaul.

Whilst on site, catapults (as well as other siege engines) would also require moving. This would have been achieved by that application of manpower, or perhaps by being dragged by mules or other pack animals. They likely were not wheeled, which would have eased their movement, and so would have been assembled where they were required and only moved when absolutely necessary. It also evidently did not occur to the Greeks to mount their artillery pieces on a cart for easy transport and rapid deployment; this innovation did not occur until the Roman period.

Rams and Ladders

As noted earlier, the traditional and simplest piece of siege technology was the scaling ladder. These were simple constructions and would have been limited in size to the height of a sapling, as these would have formed the legs of the ladder, with the steps being fastened between them. They would only have been effective, therefore, against relatively low defensive walls. The rungs would also have been of wooden construction, lashed to the frame with twine or something similar. The construction materials did not lend themselves to supporting great weight either, and perhaps only one or two soldiers could climb them at any one time. When more troops tried to access the ladders, they would easily collapse under the excess weight, as occurred at the siege of the city of the Mallians after Alexander had leapt from the wall into the city with the intention of shaming and inspiring his men to follow after a particularly lacklustre beginning to the siege. The fact that we hear of no Macedonian deaths from this collapse suggest that the ladders were of no great size. We can estimate the height of ladders at that particular siege of perhaps only 3-4m, as we also are told that some troops stood on the shoulders of their comrades in order to gain the top of the city walls. Scaling ladders must have been of poor quality indeed if they were only 3-4m high and yet still collapsed under the weight of maybe five or six soldiers.

Scaling ladders had two great advantages over other pieces of siege equipment in the ancient world, the first was that they were easy and quick to construct and did not, necessarily have to be carried from siege to siege as with catapults, siege towers and rams. The second great advantage was their flexibility and mobility of deployment. One of Alexander's hallmark strategies, as I hope to demonstrate throughout this volume and its forthcoming companion *The Field Campaigns of Alexander the Great*, was his desire and ability to attack an enemy in more than one direction simultaneously. We see this with the many flanking attacks during his set-piece battles, but also during his siege operations. At Gaza, for example, he was concentrating his attention against one section of walls, but used ladders and catapults to attack at other points to prevent the defenders concentrating in the main sector. We see the same at Tyre where he used ship-borne artillery to attack all around the city in order to achieve the same effect. Scaling ladders made this tactic eminently possible during Alexander's career as a besieger.

Their ease of construction, tactical flexibility and rapidity of deployment made scaling ladders an integral part of almost all of Alexander's sieges. Although they were seldom the primary means of victory, they did still have a role to play in the new world that Alexander had created for besieging armies. The very fact that they were used at almost every siege (with the exception of the mountain top sieges on the northeast frontier and some of the early Indian sieges) suggests strongly that defensive walls in the ancient world were almost exclusively small, otherwise ladders would not have reached the top.

Another traditional siege device was the battering ram. It was not always possible to get over any given wall with ladders, or even with siege towers, and so the option of breaking through the wall was developed. The battering ram, as with the scaling ladder, was not a new creation of the great Macedonian engineers, but had been in existence for as long as there had been siege warfare.

The simplest form of battering ram would have been a log carried by a number of men on either side that would have been used to pound a gate or doorway. It is unlikely that such a device would have had much impact against even the most primitive city walls and the force that a handful of men could impart would have been minimal, although enough to eventually break through a wooden door. This form of the weapon would also have been very exposed to missile fire from above as the defenders would have reacted to its presence. These early rams were relatively easily to counter by the defenders, and developments were fairly rapid.

The next stage of development from this simple device would have been to suspend the ram, which likely would still have been a felled tree, from a wooden frame. This frame would then be pushed into position, the ram drawn back and released. Gravity would then take over and the ram would effectively drop towards the walls or gate of the fortress under attack. The force applied to the walls would be directly proportional to the distance the ram was drawn back and upwards (and to the weight of the ram). An alternative to this moveable frame would be for a fixed scaffolding framework to be constructed against the wall or gate from which the ram would again be suspended, exactly the same principle but a fixed device rather than a moveable one. This suspended ram design would represent a development in terms of the force able to be applied to the walls by the ram, but with either of these suspended ram options, the same problem would remain; missile fire from the defenders. The men involved in operating this ram would be terribly exposed, and surely the construction crews charged with creating the scaffold if the device were fixed would have found it almost impossible to complete their work; attrition must have been very high for these men.

By the mid fourth century, these defensive deficiencies in ram technology had been addressed. From this point, battering rams were transported within wheeled sheds to protect the operators from missile fire from above. These sheds would then be simply pushed into action against the wall or gateway as required. These mobile sheds could also double as moat-filling sheds to protect work parties, although this was never required by Alexander. This work would have been facilitated by the fact that the shed would have been a basic frame only, and it would have had no floor. This meant that filling in a moat was easy work, and also that the shed could be pushed from inside by the workmen while still being protected, and not from outside where they would have been vulnerable. This shed is an extremely simple device and would be proof against light missiles; large rocks would likely have gone straight through, especially if dropped from any great height. They would also have been vulnerable to fire arrows, and would likely have been covered with hides to reduce this risk.

A further type of ram employed by Alexander was of a simple design, with the ram being mounted on wheels; this could be pushed with great speed against the walls or gates, but was still vulnerable to missile attack from above. This would have been quick to construct in the field and may have been effective against disorganised defenders; the walls could be engaged and the ram withdrawn before they could react effectively and pour fire upon the crews. If a number of such devices were strategically positioned around the circuit of a fortress, a particular crew could attack from any direction, strike the walls or doors briefly and withdraw.

The defenders also had a few techniques in their armoury for dealing with rams; it was common practice to drop large objects into their path, such as boulders or sacks of sawdust. This would delay the approach of the ram and allow the defenders time to bombard it before it could do any damage. A popular tactic was to use grappling hooks attached to ropes to snag the wooden ram and render the weapon utterly ineffective. The defenders always had the last resort of a sally in order to try and burn the siege engines of the attacker. This was a tactic used to great effect against Alexander at Halicarnassus and again at Tyre by means of the fire ship.

Siege Towers

Before the invention of the siege tower, the best, and really the only way for a besieging soldier to get onto the battlements was by using a scaling ladder, as noted earlier. These, of course, were flimsy and prone to collapse, and even when they were of sufficient quality they could not deliver more than one man at a time, which the defenders could easily deal with. Attacking armies needed a way of getting larger numbers of men onto the walls of a fortress, whilst still protecting them from missile fire as they climbed. The first siege towers did exactly that; they were essentially fortified ladders. The siege tower was first introduced to the pages of history at the siege of Motya in 398, here Diodorus describes:[29]

> He [Dionysius of Syracuse] advanced war machines of every kind against the walls and kept hammering the towers with his battering-rams, while with the catapults he kept down the fighters on the battlements; and he

also advanced against the walls his wheeled towers, six stories high, which he had built to equal the height of the houses.

As with most new technologies the siege tower is introduced in our sources without fanfare. This is no doubt because whatever the new technology, it tended to be commonplace at the time of writing; this is certainly true of siege towers for Diodorus when he was writing in the first century BC. The first siege towers, then, were wheeled for ease of movement up to the battlements; exactly what provided the propulsive force is less certain. The primary function of this particular tower (and the many more that followed it in later years) was to provide an enclosed space for the scaling ladders, to enable troops to climb to the level of the battlements without fear of missile attack from the defenders on the ramparts as they ascended. The tower also, therefore, needed some form of drawbridge that could be lowered from one of the upper stories to allow the attackers to cross from the tower to the battlements *en masse*.

Siege towers were a far more flexible weapon than this, however. Soon after the siege of Motya, the two new technologies began to be brought together; towers and catapults. Their very size made siege towers an ideal platform for catapults and archers to reign down suppressing fire upon the walls that would scatter the defenders and allow large numbers of men to gain access to the battlements before they had to fight. This was yet another advantage over scaling ladders, as with them only one man at a time could be deployed and easily attacked at a significant disadvantage as he dismounted the ladder.

The height of siege towers was only limited by the technology being employed by their builders. The first at Motya was, as Diodorus describes, six stories. The towers that Philip II employed at Perinthus in 341 were apparently 80 cubits (37m).[30] The most impressive siege towers of our period of study were those built by Alexander at Tyre which were taller than the walls of Tyre themselves, the walls being a reputed 45m. Alexander's towers were also, apparently, well stocked with siege artillery and protected against fire by flame retardant animal skins. The very size of these towers (Alexander constructed two of them on his mole), are a tremendous testimony to the construction skills of Alexander's engineers. The towers were no doubt huge, although 45m seems unbelievable, and they would have been extremely heavy. The fact that they were built, under fire from the defenders, on a mole half a mile out to sea is remarkable; the fact that the mole was solid enough to support them is even more so.

We do have surviving instructions from the ancient world as to the construction of the great engineer, Diades' towers; these instructions survive in the writings of Athenaeus, Vitruvius and the Anonymous Byzantine Historian's work entitled *Siegecraft Instructions*. We are told Diades wrote about two general sizes of siege tower, the smallest was 60 cubits high (26.6m) with a base of 17 cubits (7.5m) tapering up its height so that its highest story was 13.5 cubits (6m). This engine was 10 stories high and had a system of internal landings, rather than platforms, to support a staircase; we do not know how many men could be contained within this structure safely, but it must have been very many indeed. The larger of Diades's towers was apparently 120 cubits high (53.2m) with a base of 23.5 cubits (10.4m) tapering to 19 cubits (8.4m) at the top of its unbelievable 20 stories.[31] Diades also recommended that siege towers be covered in animal hide to prevent the obvious defensive tactic of using fire arrows against towers.

We do not have any preserved information regarding the drawbridge or how it was lowered, nor the construction technique required to provide sufficient structural integrity to support the many heavily-armed soldiers that crossed it. We know from Alexander's career that it was easy to misjudge this, as at Massaga, where many men fell from the drawbridge as it collapsed under their weight, brutally exposing them to missile fire as they lay injured on the ground some way below. Neither do we have any preserved information regarding the base of these towers. We do not know, for example, if it was exposed to the earth, or had a wooden base, making it similar to the other levels. We are told by the Anonymous Byzantine Historian that the smaller of Diades' towers had six wheels, whilst the larger had eight.

The method of propulsion is also unknown; Xenophon records a three story tower being dragged into position by a team of oxen, but this is a battlefield tower and was not being utilized in a siege situation.[32] The tower would have been dragged to a position just behind the main line and used as missile support; catapults and archers could have been stationed on each of its three stories to provide maximum firepower for the space it occupied. Firing down upon an enemy is always tactically advantageous too. This is an extremely interesting tactical device, and one that could have had great effectiveness in some defensive battlefield situations. Darius showed himself capable of using earlier technology in battle by using the, by-then-outdated chariot at Gaugamela. It would have been a very effective weapon for him if these mobile battlefield towers had been employed during his essentially-defensive battles against Alexander. There was no danger of the Persians advancing beyond the towers' effective range, certainly at the Granicus and Issus as they were set up to defend a river; a few mobile towers stationed at intervals along a river bank could have created great difficulty for Alexander and it would have been interesting to have seen how he dealt with that unique situation.

The team of oxen that pulled Cyrus' tower, as described by Xenophon, could easily have been moved out of harm's way once the tower was in position. They would not have been dragging it onto the battlefield under enemy fire. This latter point would be the main problem with using oxen, or any pack animal, to drag a tower up close to a wall; they would present an easy and obvious target for the defenders' missiles. The Goths discovered this in 537 AD during their siege of Rome. Procopius tells us:[33]

> On the eighteenth day from the beginning of the siege the Goths moved against the fortifications at about sunrise and all the Romans were struck with consternation at the sight of the advancing towers and rams, with which they were altogether unfamiliar. But Belisarius, seeing the ranks of the enemy as they advanced with the engines, began to laugh, and commanded the soldiers to remain quiet and under no circumstances to begin fighting until he himself should give the signal.

At the word of command, the Roman defenders showered missiles down upon the oxen and disabled the siege towers. We do not hear of this occurring to any of Alexander's siege towers during any of his sieges, and so must conclude that they were not drawn by teams of pack animals.

In all likelihood, Alexander's towers were propelled in a two-fold manner. Firstly, they probably had no floors; this enabled the men inside to stand on the ground and push the tower forward. To enable enough men to push at any given time, a number of crossbars would have been constructed from left to right across the base, against which men would push. The Greeks for a very long time had also had knowledge of the principle of a pulley system to provide a propulsive force; it is easy to imagine a larger number of men positioned behind the towers and pulling on ropes whose pulley would probably have been driven into the ground in front of the tower. A large number of men would, therefore, have been able to pull/push the tower simultaneously forwards towards the fortification. Those inside the tower were obviously protected from the wooden superstructure, while those behind would have been largely protected by the tower itself; missiles fired at an angle could still have reached them, however, once they came within range. It may be that those on the pulley stopped pulling once they got within missile range of the defenders. In order for this system to be effective, the tower would not have contained any men other than those pushing/pulling whilst it was being manoeuvred into position. Any excess weight, like this, would have been eliminated to make the task more manageable with as few men as possible (space within the tower would have been limited too). It is likely that those attacking over the bridge in the towers would have been Hypaspists or Agrianians, specialist troops. The archers were there to denude the battlements of defenders in order to allow the assault troops to gain a foothold.

There is no direct evidence for the use of a pulley system, but we can be reasonably certain that oxen were not used, as Alexander never had difficulty in getting his towers into position, and manpower is the only other real alternative. Space inside would have been restricted, making a secondary propulsion system necessary. We also have to bear in mind that the majority of Alexander's siege towers were not as large as those described by Diades. At Tyre, his siege towers were undoubtedly huge, but they were fixed in position on the mole, rather than wheeled – the risk of them being pulled or falling into the sea would have been too great for them to have been wheeled. The Tyrians may well have tried to secure ropes to them and drag them, using ships, into the sea if they had not been fixed. Alexander's towers that were constructed during later sieges on the northeast frontier and in India would have been rather small. We can presume this from the fact that at Massaga the drawbridge broke as the Macedonians were trying to cross, yet we hear of none of them dying from the fall, casualties came as a result of enemy fire as they lay on the ground. The walls, and thus the tower, can not have been very high if the fall was not severe enough to kill. We also know at the city of the Mallians that, after the ladders broke under the weight of hypaspists trying to climb up them to help Alexander, several troops reached the top of the ramparts by standing on the shoulders of a colleague, again telling us that the walls were not tall and thus the towers (where appropriate) would not have needed to be anything like as large as those Diades describes, or as those built at Tyre.

The potential operational use of siege towers made them a perfect weapon for Alexander's general tactic of attacking an enemy in multiple directions simultaneously. This is a tactic that we see Alexander repeating at every possible opportunity from the sieges of Halicarnassus and Tyre, to the great set-piece battles described in the subsequent volume of this work. At every military encounter where this tactic was possible, large or small, Alexander employed it. One of the great disadvantages of a besieger before the invention of the catapult, and the widespread use of siege towers, was that the defenders could quite easily concentrate their fire against attackers in a relatively small area. Troops climbing ladders could easily be countered, with the result noted above that earlier sieges were almost never successfully carried out by the attacker unless the defenders were betrayed or surrendered because of starvation or thirst.

Siege towers were not invincible, however, as Alexander was to discover several times. At Halicarnassus, Alexander had evidently not taken the advice of Diades regarding protecting towers with animal hides. The defenders, led by Ephialtes, realizing the danger posed by Alexander's towers and other siege engines, made a sally from the city and succeeded in causing great damage to Alexander's siege capability, including the destruction of one tower and a number of catapults. Uncharacteristically for Alexander, he made seemingly the same mistake again at Tyre where the Tyrians made clever use of the device of the fire ship to destroy his towers at the end of the growing mole.[34] Alexander had not protected them with skins again (he did so for the giant towers he constructed after this). This mistake is likely out of Alexander's arrogance in simply not seeing how defenders, stuck inside a fortress half a mile out to sea, could possibly hope to sortie against his siege engines with any success. Their destruction at Tyre was a huge setback to Alexander, and depressed him greatly. After a period of contemplation, he resolved to rebuild the mole even larger than before (it had been damaged by a storm too), and to construct giant towers upon it; Alexander never accepted a setback for long. The incident also made him realize his absolute need for a fleet in order to carry the city, as will be discussed later.

Alexander used siege towers to the pinnacle of their operational effectiveness. They spread out the defenders by allowing him to more effectively attack a number of different wall sections simultaneously, and they allowed him to lay down a suppressing fire against the defenders on the ramparts. The coupling of catapults with siege towers led to even greater effectiveness and, together with Alexander's natural genius for siege technique, led to Alexander being almost invincible in the art of siege warfare.

Siege towers were not restricted to the aggressors in a siege. We see at Halicarnassus and again at Tyre, the defenders made use of siege towers to perform exactly the same role as did the attackers. The defenders in these two instances realized the potential of the besieger's siege towers raining down missiles onto their ramparts, and indeed within the city, with impunity. The defenders attempted to construct their own towers to be even higher than the attackers, to turn the tables on them, as it were.[35] This was an excellent defensive tactic, the fact that it ultimately failed should not detract from its inventiveness. It also implies that constructing the simplest form of fixed tower (they would have had no cause to include wheels) was perhaps no great engineering feat as the defenders of these two cities probably did not have access to the finest engineering minds that Greece had to offer, as Alexander did.

Sapping

Sapping was another traditional siege technique that required no developments in technology to make it possible. This technique involved digging a tunnel underneath a section of wall or a tower, at a relatively shallow depth. This tunnel would be supported by wooden struts at regular intervals, as with a more typical mine shaft. Once the tunnel had been extended underneath the walls, the struts would be set on fire and the ceiling would, in theory, collapse, along with the wall above it. The depth of the digging operation was critical, if the tunnel was dug too deep, the tunnel walls may support the weight even after the struts were burned, and it may not collapse at all. If the tunnel was too shallow then the weight of the walls above ground may collapse the tunnel even before the struts were fired.

Sapping had a number of fundamental drawbacks. Tunnelling was inherently dangerous for the miners; tunnels could collapse prematurely if not properly supported (and even despite that on occasion), killing the miners. It may have been difficult to get enough oxygen into the mine to properly burn the wooden struts; if they did not burn properly, the miners could not safely return to the mine to finish the job, as they would almost certainly have burned enough to become unstable. This could be likened to returning to a firework that did not ignite correctly. The most obviously fundamental drawback of sapping was terrain; the topography had to be correct for it to even be attempted. Fortresses that sat upon solid rock were impervious to this technique, whilst those on terrain that was too soft (i.e. swampy terrain or perhaps very fine sand; Gaza was evidently more solid than this) were equally safe.

There were also a number of key advantages to this technique. The minors were protected from attack by the tunnel itself, much in the same way that a siege tower protected those within. The defenders could do little to stop sapping operations, except deal with the consequences in terms of building extra internal walls to protect the city when a breach was formed. Walls could also be brought down from scratch in a relatively short period of time; some of Alexander's Indian sieges imply that sapping operations had achieved a measure of success after only a few days to a week.

Alexander proved himself to be adept at this form of siegecraft. It was not typically employed on the Greek mainland due to the difficulties of the terrain, but Alexander employed the technique wherever he could. The sources first tell us of Alexander conducting sapping operations during the siege of Gaza in 332. Little is actually recorded save that the operation seems to have begun behind a section of Alexander's circumvallation in order to hide the fact that these operations were underway. It is hard to see why Alexander felt the need to hide his operations, given that the defenders could do little about them anyway. The Gaza sapping operation was a particular success, although it received only the briefest of mentions in Diodorus. Arrian tells us:[36]

> Saps were dug at various points, the earth being removed unobserved by the enemy, until in many places the wall, having nothing to support it, collapsed and fell.

The very fact that Gaza's walls were sapped decries the idea that the city sat upon a mound; it is certainly true that today the city does indeed sit upon such a mound, but this is the collected detritus of millennia and was not present in 332. The sands of the desert upon which Gaza sat were an ideal terrain for Alexander to try this new technique, and he was evidently delighted with the results. Having said this, he still had to wait many years before he could repeat this tactic. He did not conduct another siege operation of any kind until he was in the northeast frontier region, and there every citadel seemed to be sited on a mountain top where sapping was obviously impractical. Once Alexander entered India he was able to conduct such operations at a series of sites including Sangala and Massaga. With hindsight, sapping was not critical in the capture of these cities as they were relatively minor fortifications in comparison with the might of Tyre, Gaza and Halicarnassus. Gaza was the only instance in Alexander's career, therefore, where sapping was instrumental in capturing the city; in every other case we could quite easily argue that he would have been successful even without sapping. All it could have done, and this is valuable in itself, was perhaps reduce the length of the siege by a few days at best, and thus perhaps save lives.

Naval Siege Equipment

One of Alexander's great skills as a strategist and tactician was his ability to adapt to new circumstances and environments. During the siege of Halicarnassus he used the catapult against walls for the first time in history (or perhaps the second if he had done so at Miletus a few weeks previously); these were an existing weapon of war being used in a new way, to directly assault a fortifications wall. Alexander saw the potential of these weapons and embraced them eagerly in a way earlier generals simply had not. He was never one to sit on his laurels, however; new challenges and situations were always presenting themselves, and exactly that occurred at Tyre in 332.

As will be noted at various times, one of Alexander's hallmark strategies was to attack an opponent in multiple directions simultaneously. He achieved this by a series of flanking attacks during his set-piece battles, and by using catapults, towers, rams and scaling ladders to attack various points along the walls of defensive positions (as far as was practicable). At Tyre, however, Alexander encountered an entirely new situation; the fortress was built on an island half a mile out to sea. After the disbanding of the majority of his fleet at Halicarnassus, he possessed no ships with which to harass the walls that faced out to sea. His initial reaction was still to attack (as always), but his inability to prevent Tyrian naval sorties against his working parties, and against his siege towers on the mole, made this tactic extremely difficult, if not close to impossible. The fleet of Tyre was fairly strong, and certainly far greater than the few Athenian transport vessels Alexander still possessed. The Persian fleet was also not yet subdued and theoretically on the side of Tyre – at least by the default of using the principle that my enemy's enemy is my friend. As long as these two situations prevailed (Alexander's lack of a fleet and the Tyrian possession of one) then Alexander's continued assault on Tyre was in jeopardy. We are told that Alexander seriously contemplated abandoning the siege at least once. The real issue for Alexander was being restricted to a single avenue of attack – the mole.

Alexander's solution was twofold – firstly he realized that he needed to acquire a fleet. With this intention, he set off north to Byblos and Sidon to essentially take possession of their fleets once their respective kings had returned to those cities, having been at sea at the time they fell into Alexander's hands. Alexander's triumphant return to Tyre at the head of this newly-acquired fleet was the turning point in the siege, and allowed the implementation of his second tactical development.

Even with a new fleet, Alexander realized that he would only be able to suppress Tyrian naval sorties, he would not actually be able to go the extra step of actually attacking the city anywhere around its circuit except for the section directly opposite the mole. Alexander therefore began to experiment with using siege engines at sea by stationing them on board his naval vessels. The first device was simple enough, to position some catapults onboard a number of triremes and to station them close enough to the walls to assault them directly. This would have entailed adding to, or at least solidifying, the deck to give them a solid base from which to fire. These catapults were evidently both arrow-throwing and stone-throwing varieties, the former for suppression of the defenders, the latter for penetration of the walls. We know that this simple innovation was effective, as the defenders had to drop rocks into the sea to try to prevent the ships from drawing too close, and had divers cut the mooring ropes of the vessels that were preparing to fire; they would not have acted to counter this attack if it was not having some effect.

Alexander's second naval siege weapon was far more innovative; he apparently had pairs of triremes lashed together at their prows, again with special decks constructed between them. Upon these decks were stationed a naval version of a siege tower. These ships, lashed as they were, would have formed something of a delta shape with a deck extending between the two ships, and the tower precariously supported on it above the water.[37] This arrangement seems remarkably unstable, and surely could not have supported a particularly tall tower, or for that matter many assault troops within it. Having said this, missiles launched from even a two or three story tower were more likely to have an impact upon the defenders than arrows launched from sea level. These naval towers may well have also had a psychological impact on the defenders due to the entire city now coming under attack, rather than just one small, easily-defensible section.

This ship-borne artillery and the siege towers were intended to act in coordination with marines (who were the ever-versatile hypaspists) on troop transport vessels. These troop ships would have been equipped with scaling ladders that were raised from a turret, not unlike the larger naval siege towers. The general tactic was for the artillery and archers to lay down a suppressing fire against the defenders on the walls and clear an area which would allow the marines to climb the walls unhindered. The fact that the hypaspists were able to climb the walls using ladders, rather than large siege towers, strongly implies that the walls away from the landward side of the fortress were of considerable smaller dimensions. When Tyre was built, nobody would have imagined a concerted attack by sea against anything other than the two harbours; firstly because of its technical difficulty, secondly the ease with which it could be repelled (except for the actions of the artillery of course) and thirdly the strength of the Tyrian and Persian navies.

It is a sobering thought that all of the effort, man-power and raw materials that went into the construction of the mole and the siege towers upon it, actually did not cause the fall of the city; the breakthrough was made by the hypaspists attacking (from the sea) a collapsed section of wall that had been brought down by naval catapults. This is superficially true, but would be slightly missing the point, however. The mole and its towers kept a very large number of the defenders busy while the hypaspists were affecting their breakthrough of the fallen section of wall. Alexander's tactic of attacking from multiple directions simultaneously had again proved a success. We should not forget the fact, however, that Alexander's engineers were just as important, if not more so, in the fall of Tyre than were the rest of the army, as they made every offensive action against the city possible.

Chapter 2

Pellium and Thebes: 335

Introduction

When Philip II, the father of Alexander the Great, succeeded to the throne of Macedonia in 359, he inherited a kingdom beset by enemies on all sides. Within the first year of his reign, by a combination of guile and military inventiveness, he had defeated the immediate Illyrian threat and secured Macedonia's borders. For the rest of his life, some twenty-three years, Philip campaigned almost constantly to create a Macedonia that was the most powerful nation in the Greek world. This was a campaign, or more accurately a series of them, that culminated in victory at Chaeronea in 338; a battle which effectively ended Greek freedom and independence. At the league of Corinth, an organization set up by Philip shortly afterwards as a means of controlling the Greek states, Philip was elected *hegemon*, essentially captain-general of Greece. Never before had any Greek, let alone a Macedonian, held so much power, power that Alexander undoubtedly envied during Philip's lifetime.

When Philip was assassinated in the summer of 336 by a Macedonian soldier called Pausanias, probably motivated by a personal grudge against the king, the Greek world, including Macedonia, was briefly thrown into turmoil.[38] The Greek city states had been forced into submission by Philip using a combination of politics, threats and military defeats. Philip's death, after a hard fought, long and bloody war, was viewed by men like Demosthenes of Athens as an opportunity to make one last grab for freedom. These men longed for a return to the golden age of Greece, where they were free to decide their own fate without having to appease a semi-barbarous (in their view) foreign despot. They no doubt attempted to view Macedonia's rise to power in its historical context: many of the city states had, for a short time, exercised a measure of control over their neighbours; the most recent example being Thebes soon after the end of the Peloponnesian War. The Greeks would remember that as soon as Epaminondas and Pelopidas, the architects of Thebes' rise to power, were dead, Thebes quickly fell from dominance. The city states had every reason to expect the same to happen to Macedonia; there could have been no doubt in their minds that its rise was due almost entirely to Philip. Their views would have been further confirmed by his successor, the young Alexander. The city states would have seen him as an unknown and untried beardless youth of barely 20 years, hardly a man to fear. They would, however, very quickly learn their mistake: it had taken Philip over twenty years to subdue the city states; it took Alexander less than two.

Alexander's succession to the throne of Macedonia was far from a certainty; Philip had not himself been the rightful heir, but initially took power as regent for Amyntas, the young son of Perdiccas, the former king. Given the state of the kingdom that Philip inherited, the throne must have seemed like something of a poisoned chalice; his success in quickly securing Macedonia's borders led to him keeping the throne even when Amyntas passed an age where he would have been considered competent to rule. Macedonian kingship was not hereditary, and simply being son of the former king did not automatically confer the throne upon you (as in the case of Amyntas), but it did make you a strong contender (as with Alexander).

It was the Macedonian army assembly that had the power to decide who was to become the next king. By a skilful use of political assassination, persuasive oratory and behind the scenes deals in which the key power brokers in Macedonian were brought to Alexander's flag (men like Parmenio, Antipater and Alexander of Lyncestis), Alexander was confirmed king. For Alexander, the timing of the Persian expedition launched by Philip was critical, Amyntas and Parmenio were in Asia Minor at the time of the assassination, and Amyntas was not fully able, therefore, to muster the support that he may have been able to if he had been at court. In this, as so often throughout Alexander's career, the gods were smiling on the young king.

Parmenio was probably the single most important political figure in Macedonia, apart from the king, during the reign of Philip; this is also true during the early part of Alexander's reign. He, as well as various family members, was well entrenched at court and seems to have had political connections with both factions contending for the succession in the final years of Philip's reign (and immediately after his assassination). Thus when Philip was assassinated, Parmenio was in a prime position to act as king-maker. He was in a position to offer the support of most of the lowland barons; this would leave Amyntas, or any other potential rival, with only the possibility of forming a coalition of fringe areas of Macedonia and of rebellious Greek cities. Parmenio was evidently a skilled political operator and knew well the strength of his position and what his support was worth, as Alexander would soon discover.

Immediately upon his succession, Alexander began a series of all-too-predictable purges of any possible usurper, a sign of his insecurity. Large numbers died, including potential rivals like Amyntas and two of the sons of Aëropus, known supporters of Amyntas' claim; the third only being spared because of his immediate support for Alexander. The purges were to secure his throne from potential rivals, and the army had been won over by a combination of the support of senior generals and brilliant oratory, but the Macedonian people also needed to be brought on board. To this end, Alexander announced that he would rule along similar principles to his father; he even abolished taxation in order to win popular support.

Alexander had secured the throne, but at what cost? Philip had left no money in the Macedonian treasury, and Alexander's largesse at his succession, along with the remittance of taxation, left a tremendous fiscal problem. A perhaps more important issue was created within the command structure of the army; Parmenio had exacted a steep price for his support which included the assassination of Amyntas, his co-commander of the Persian expeditionary force.

Alexander was forced to pay a heavy price for Parmenio's support, but in 336 he was in no position to argue. When the Macedonian army crossed the Hellespont into Asia, almost every key command was held by one of Parmenio's sons, brothers, or some other kinsmen. Two of Parmenio's sons were commanders of the hypaspists (Nicanor) and the Companion Cavalry (Philotas); along with Parmenio himself commanding the Thessalian cavalry and essentially being second in command of the entire Macedonian army. Parmenio's brother, Asander, probably commanded the light cavalry and certainly received the satrapy of Sardis as soon as it was conquered. Parmenio's supporters were also firmly entrenched in positions of power, men like the four sons of Andromenes and the brothers Coenus and Cleander. Many of the commanders of the army of invasion were little younger than Parmenio himself: when Justin tells us that headquarters looked 'more like the senate of some old-time republic' he is probably not exaggerating in his description, although it is a far from flattering one.[39]

This was a situation which Alexander could not tolerate indefinitely. He allowed this situation to remain relatively unchanged whilst his success was still in the balance; but after Gaugamela, Alexander began to make serious and sweeping changes to the army, changes which were made considerably easier by the assassinations of both Philotas and Parmenio. It was not until the army was in India that every position was filled with 'Alexander's men' rather than Philip's (through the figure of Parmenio).

Greece

Once the deal-making and political assassinations were complete in Macedonia, or at least were well underway, Alexander's position as king was established. His difficulties did not end there, however. He could easily be removed from the throne by means of assassination, as with his father, or perhaps through civil war if he was not seen to be a strong expansionist leader the likes of which the Macedonian army had grown accustomed to in Philip; it was long established that Macedonian kings seldom died in their beds. With Macedonia now under control, Alexander needed to assert his authority on the wider Greek world, to send a message that nothing had changed except the name of the king. Alexander also needed to quell the unrest, particularly amongst his Balkan neighbours, before he could contemplate continuing the invasion of Persia that his father had started in a minor way with the expeditionary force of Parmenio and Amyntas.[40]

Alexander's Balkan campaign was punctuated by two sieges, those of Pellium and Thebes. Each of these presented Alexander with unique situations that he had not encountered before and which he had to adapt to in order to overcome the enemy.

The initial part of Alexander's first campaign as king shows little of the lightning speed for which he was later to become famous, but this is because of a desire to link up with elements of his fleet on the Danube River before he turned to the siege of Pellium. Ancient warships did not travel quickly, and so we see Alexander progressing very slowly through enemy territory so as not to be forced to stay on the banks of the Danube for several weeks exhausting the food supply of that region as he did so. Lack of food is seldom a significant problem in Alexander's career, excluding the exceptional events of the Gedrosian desert, but it was to become an issue at Pellium.

Pellium

After the initial part of his Balkan campaign to the north (described in my forthcoming book *The Field Campaigns of Alexander the Great*), Alexander began to head back towards Macedonia. He marched south from the Danube towards the Trojan pass, but instead of crossing it and heading straight back towards Macedonia, he turned southwest and made for the region of the modern day Sofia to visit with king Langaros of the Agrianians.

Whilst Alexander was visiting Langaros, he received news that three Illyrian tribes were making plans and mobilizing to attack western Macedonia; these were the Dardanians under Cleitus, the Taulantians under Glaucias, and the Autaratians. Much of the Macedonian field army was with Alexander at this time. This had left Macedonia's western borders open to ravaging by the Illyrians, which was their traditional tactic.[41] This is perhaps a foolish oversight on the part of Alexander, to leave his homeland undefended, but there are several reasons for this. Firstly, this was his opening campaign as king, and he would have wanted a massive show of force to cow Macedonia's neighbours into submission. Secondly, his position as king was still not as absolute as it was to become; keeping the whole of the army with him meant that he could keep an eye on his soldiers and prevent any potential rivals that were left alive in Macedonia from persuading part of the army that he was not the rightful heir to the throne. Whatever the reasons, the fact was that Macedonia was left almost completely undefended by Alexander's march north, and he had to act quickly to quell this growing Illyrian threat lest the Greek states to the south, or Thracian tribesmen to the east, attempt to take advantage.

We know almost nothing about Alexander's visit with Langaros, save that it lasted for some time and that, before moving west towards Pellium and the growing Illyrian threat, Alexander persuaded Langaros to deal with one of the three revolting tribes, the Autaratians, himself.[42] We know nothing at all about Langaros' campaign against the Autaratians, other than to say it was evidently highly successful, as they were never again a problem to either Alexander or Antipater, his regent once the invasion of Asia began.

The Pellium campaign lasted around two months, considerably more time than the events narrated by Arrian would appear to have taken. The only conclusion must be that the delay with Langaros, persuading him to support Alexander, took rather longer than we may have expected. Either way, it was time well spent as the Agrianians were amongst Alexander's finest troops throughout his career and were invaluable in almost every military situation, not least during his many sieges.

The deal with Langaros had been crucial in securing Alexander's flank for this march; Langaros moved west against the Autaratians at the same time Alexander was making his march, preventing any potential attack on the

Macedonian column. From the territory of the Agrianians, Alexander marched most likely via Prilep, arriving at the upper reaches of the Erigon River around Cepikovo, and then he followed the river south towards Florina and the central Lyncestis plain. There had been unrest in this area since Alexander's murder of two of the sons of Aëropus upon his succession. The route Alexander took into Lyncestis was also the route that would be taken by the Roman consul P. Sulpicius Galba in 200.[43]

Alexander arrived without incident before the gates of a city which Arrian calls Pellium; unfortunately he was too late to prevent Cleitus from occupying the city. Arrian's descriptions of Pellium and the surrounding area are too vague to allow identification, but are substantial enough to allow us to recreate the siege with a degree of certainty. We do know, however, that Pellium was on the border with Macedonia, close to the western city of Edessa, and its hostile occupation was, and would remain, a threat to the security of Macedonia's western border; something Alexander simply could not allow if his Persian expedition were to proceed. An Illyrian threat would have been a particularly sensitive issue for a Macedonian king, given the historical wars between the two areas, culminating in the death of Perdiccas III at the hands of Bardylis that precipitated Philip's reign.

Immediately upon arriving at Pellium, Alexander made camp outside of the city by the Eordiacus River, with the intention of beginning the siege of the city the following morning. Cleitus had not only occupied the city, but sensibly had also occupied the heights that ringed it to the northeast and southeast; although he did not quite have the manpower to surround the Macedonians on every side as Arrian suggests.[44] Cleitus' ridge-based troops can not have been visible in that area immediately upon Alexander's arrival on the plain, as it would have been evident that he was walking into a trap; they must have been some distance away, awaiting a prearranged signal before advancing. Despite Cleitus having occupied the city before Alexander's arrival, the Macedonians were quick enough to prevent him from linking up with his Taulantian allies, which would have been a considerably more difficult problem for Alexander to deal with. The other problem, of course, was that Alexander did not know the location of the Taulantians, or when they would arrive; ancient intelligence networks were rudimentary at best. Alexander simply had to make the most of the situation while he could, and remain flexible enough to deal with the imminent threat of a secondary column.

The city of Pellium was in a naturally-strong defensive position; it was surrounded on three sides by a heavily-wooded ridge with a plain before it. The ridge essentially formed a horseshoe with the city at the apex, and the open end leading to a narrow wooded canyon along the Eordaicus River that led to the Wolf Pass, itself only wide enough for four men to march abreast.[45]

Alexander marched the bulk of his army through the Wolf Pass, and through the wooded canyon by the Eordaicus River and into the plain before the city of Pellium. Once Alexander arrived in the plain, Cleitus brought up his Dardanians to the edge of the ridge that surrounded Alexander on three sides. The Macedonians suddenly found themselves in an extremely-difficult position and at a serious tactical disadvantage. Alexander would have been aware that one of Philip's few defeats in his entire career came in almost identical circumstances at the hands of Onomarchus of Phocis. In that instance Onomarchus had drawn Philip into a horseshoe-shaped canyon in order to unleash his catapults and other missile weapons upon him from above: this was one of the first times in Greek warfare that catapults were used as field artillery. If Cleitus had possessed artillery, Alexander could have been faced with a similar humiliating defeat, but throughout his career, Alexander was always lucky.

After what must have been a very tense night, in which Alexander would have been compelled to keep most of the army under arms in case of a night attack by the Dardanians, morning broke with the two armies in exactly the same position as they had been the previous night. Cleitus had missed two golden opportunities to bloody the collective noses of the Macedonians: he had failed to employ missile troops at a time when they could have been devastating, and failed to offer any sort of a night skirmish that would have come from three sides, which also would have been potentially devastating to the Macedonians. Even though Cleitus had failed to act decisively, the fact that Alexander was forced to keep his troops under arms meant that they would have been tired, and in theory at a disadvantage the following morning. It was only then that Cleitus chose to act.

Once Cleitus did decide to make his move, his actions were so negative as to surrender his main advantage; that of having the Macedonians surrounded. Cleitus feigned an attack upon the Macedonians in which there was very little fighting, and he withdrew his troops stationed along the ridge, within the walls of the city. Cleitus evidently felt little confidence in the quality of his own troops, as compared to the Macedonians; coupled with the fact that Glaucias had not yet arrived with the anticipated reinforcements, defence became the preferred strategy.

After Cleitus had withdrawn within the protection of the city walls, Alexander had a perfect opportunity to assault the city before any reinforcements could arrive and potentially alter the balance of power. The fact that apparently all of Cleitus' troops were able to be garrisoned within Pellium rather suggests that their force was not particularly large as Pellium was certainly nowhere near the size of the great Greek cities like Athens or Thebes. We must ask why Alexander failed to take advantage of the opportunity to assault the city immediately. The answer is not difficult to find: throughout the period prior to Alexander's career the defenders always held the advantage in any siege. We see during the Peloponnesian War, for example, the Spartans reluctant or perhaps unable to conduct any sort of significant siege of Athens, despite having numerous opportunities to do so. They contented themselves with trying to force a hoplite battle - which of course the Athenians consistently refused - and to ravaging the Attic countryside. The real reason for this defensive advantage was the relative lack of effective siege equipment; catapults were a recent invention, as discussed above, and were only just working their way into Greek warfare. Stone-throwing catapults were revolutionary when they were first introduced in 334. The besiegers were usually reduced to the use of ladders and rams, and frequently to reliance upon deception and betrayal from within for a city to fall without the application of force.

Alexander's force at Pellium was relatively small, and although the troops were of undoubted quality, there was no siege train and therefore even the limited siege equipment available at the time was not available to Alexander. Without the ability to assault the city, and lacking in Phillip's guile and cunning that may have led to the city being betrayed to him, Alexander had only one real option: to blockade the city. In order to achieve an effective blockade, Alexander built a circumvallation around its walls. The circumvallation can not have been particularly high, as Arrian tells us that 'on the following day Glaucias appeared with a large force'.[46] Glaucias' arrival again put Alexander in a perilous position. Glaucias positioned his force of Taulantians across the mountain pass that Alexander had used to enter the plain before Pellium; this had the effect of cutting Alexander's lines of supply and communication back to Macedonia, as well as giving Alexander no possibility of a safe withdrawal. With retreat out of the question, and any attack on Pellium likely to be costly in manpower given the lack of siege equipment and the likelihood of a flanking attack from Glaucias, Alexander's position was extremely difficult. If Alexander had known of the imminent arrival of Glaucias then his decision to advance upon Pellium and build the circumvallation was a significant tactical mistake. He should have withdrawn through the pass and formulated another strategy. If he had not known of Glaucias' movements, this is an excellent example of the poor quality of military intelligence in the ancient world; that such a large force operating close by, and whose arrival on the scene was imminent, was utterly unknown to Alexander.

Alexander had almost certainly begun the Pellium campaign expecting it to be brief; the city would be captured and the local tribesmen forced into submission without much difficulty. Along with this expectation, Alexander had begun the expedition with only basic supplies, expecting to be able to live off the land for the brief time he would be in the Balkans. The arrival of Glaucias caused two significant logistical problems for Alexander. Firstly, he needed to be able to send out foraging parties to gather the food and water needed to keep the army supplied. Secondly, he needed to be able to graze the pack animals. The very presence of pack animals is a clear shift in organizational policy from Philip's reign, he had reduced the size of the baggage train massively and pack animals were rarely used.

These two key logistical requirements forced Alexander to risk detaching the baggage animals to the nearby plain of Korce, some 8km to the northwest of the city. The baggage animals were accompanied by Philotas and a group of cavalry to act as a guard and, presumably, to double as a foraging expedition.[47] This foraging expedition was a significant risk for Alexander, and illustrates that supplies must have been running very low indeed.

When Glaucias saw the column setting off for grazing lands, he seized the opportunity to force a confrontation: he detached a portion of his troops to occupy the high ground surrounding the plain that Philotas was heading for. When the danger to the foraging expedition that resulted from Glaucias' movements was reported back to Alexander, he took the Agrianians, hypaspists, archers and 400 cavalry and advanced quickly on Philotas' new position. Upon seeing their approach, Glaucias decided not to risk a battle, and withdrew his troops to their former positions. The baggage animals were then safely escorted back to the plain of Pellium by Alexander's larger escort force. It is unclear as to the level of success of their expedition, but given its brevity it seems unlikely that much forage was gathered.

The foraging expedition had been a tremendous risk by Alexander, and shows the desperate nature of his situation; it was also a situation that could have been better exploited by Glaucias. It would have taken at least a couple of hours for Alexander's relief force to have reached a plain 8km distance from Pellium; this should have been enough time for Glaucias' advance force to have at least harassed, and perhaps directly engaged, the Macedonians. Coupled with this was the possibility of both Glaucias and Cleitus' failure to attack the remnants of the Macedonian force that were left in the plain of Pellium when Alexander set off to relieve Philotas. Many key troops had been taken by Alexander, and we can only guess at the chaos that could have resulted from a two-pronged attack from front and rear by both Glaucias and Cleitus on those who remained, without the guiding hand of Alexander being present.

Following the probable failure of the foraging mission, Alexander's logistical situation was becoming increasingly desperate, and he was still essentially surrounded on the plain before Pellium. If he were to attempt a direct withdrawal then he would almost certainly have to fight his way out at a significant tactical disadvantage, along with the likelihood of being attacked in the flank and rear as he did so. Alexander's only option was to come up with some sort of ruse to clear the surrounding foothills of defenders before he made his escape.

Alexander's solution was an incredible display of parade ground drill, described by Arrian:[48]

> Alexander drew up the main body of his infantry in mass formation 120 deep, posting on either wing 200 cavalrymen with instructions to make no noise, and to obey orders smartly. Then he gave the order for the heavy infantry first to erect their spears, and afterwards, at the word of command, to lower the massed points as for attack, swinging them, again at the word of command, now to the right, now to the left. The whole phalanx he then moved smartly forward, and, wheeling it this way and that, caused it to execute various intricate movements. Having thus put his troops with great rapidity through a number of different formations, he ordered his left to form a wedge and advance to the attack.

The Taulantians had been drawn onto the plain during the manoeuvres, for reasons that are not altogether clear. After this brief display of drill, Alexander's troops formed up into the wedge formation and advanced upon them. This incredible display of discipline conducted initially in absolute silence, save for the shouting of orders, struck fear into the untrained Taulantians to such an extent that they broke without a fight and fled the field in confusion.

A small number of evidently more hardy Taulantians remained in the hills overlooking the pass through which Alexander had entered the plain, and through which he planned to leave. In order to drive out the remnants of Glaucias' Taulantians, Alexander attacked with the hypaspists, Agrianians, archers and Companion Cavalry. The decision to use the Companions to assault a defensive position in the hills on either side of a pass is curious, particularly with Arrian's reference to half of them being ordered to dismount and fight on foot: either the pass was not as mountainous as we may believe, or Alexander wanted to attack them without any delay, and cavalry would reach them faster than infantry; I assume the latter.[49] Alexander probably wanted to ensure that the defenders were dislodged by the time the infantry reached the pass, and the only way to engage them quickly was by using the cavalry in this unorthodox manner. The Companions were not required to actually engage the remaining defenders as they fled further into the mountains at the approach of Alexander's elite cavalry units.

With the Companions occupying the hills, the Agrianians, hypaspists and archers set up a defensive position on the Pellium side of the river to cover the retreat of the remainder of the heavy infantry across the river and back through the Wolf Pass. With the Macedonians essentially in retreat, at least from the perspective of Cleitus and Glaucias, the natives were able to join forces and advance upon the rear of the Macedonian column. The heavy infantry units evidently crossed the river before the Dardanians and Taulantians could engage them, and made it through the Wolf Pass without incident. The Agrianians, archers, hypaspists and Companions who had set up a defensive position, however, now came under pressure from the advancing native tribesmen. These troops then conducted an orderly withdrawal under cover of archer fire and javelins thrown by the Agrianians. Alexander's artillery were also set up along the far bank of the river to further provided covering fire. This artillery was with the siege train that was evidently on its way to Pellium, but had not arrived in time to be used against the city. The catapults were evidently arrow-throwing and not terribly effective as anti-personnel weapons, but the fear that they inspired was far more significant; the natives refused to come within range of the weapons, despite their relative ineffectiveness. The fighting withdrawal across the river is a superb example of such an operation; Alexander was able to extricate himself from the failed siege with no loss of life by a combination of leadership, the discipline of his troops, and tactical inventiveness. This was only the second incident in history of artillery being used to support a field operation, the first being their use against Philip by Onomarchus of Phocis in 354, noted above.

Once safely across the river, Alexander moved his troops several miles from the pass, with the intention of tricking Cleitus and Glaucias into believing that he was retreating back to the safety of Macedonia. Once at a reasonable distance, the Macedonians made camp and sent out several reconnaissance parties to establish whether they were being followed, and to see how their opponents had responded to their withdrawal. Arrian tells us that after three days these scouts reported back that the Dardanians and Taulantians were celebrating their apparent victory and were drinking heavily. They had also extended their lines dangerously, no palisade or trench had been constructed and no sentries posted; so convinced were they that Alexander had been completely defeated and was long gone from the region.[50]

As soon as he received the news, Alexander reformed a column of troops consisting of the hypaspists, Agrianians, archers and two *taxeis* of *pezhetairoi* (Perdiccas and Coenus). This advance column was followed at a slower pace by the remainder of the army. Under cover of night, the column marched back through the Wolf Pass and crossed the River Eordaicus without interference. The moment was ripe for an attack, and without waiting for the rest of his force to be brought up with the possibility of losing the element of surprise if he were to be discovered, Alexander immediately ordered the Agrianians and archers to make a surprise assault across a narrow front. Many of the Illyrian tribesmen were either killed in their beds or cut down whilst fleeing in panic at the unexpected turn of events. The attack was pressed by all members of the advanced column and Arrian tells us that the only way the defenders escaped was to abandon their weapons.[51] Cleitus and what remained of the Dardanian force fled into the relative security of the fortress of Pellium, whilst Glaucias and the Taulantians evidently fled into the mountains, a broken force.

Alexander reformed his forces and advanced upon Pellium, this time not to be denied. Cleitus, evidently seeing the impossibility of his situation, with no likelihood of a relief column to assist, set fire to the city and abandoned it, seeking refuge with Glaucias in the mountains.

The Pellium campaign gives us our first opportunity to examine Alexander's abilities in the art of siegecraft, and in a number of ways he was found wanting. Alexander committed a serious tactical error in not taking with him sufficient provisions to allow him to conduct the siege; this was compounded by the fact that he allowed himself to become surrounded by the Dardanians and the Taulantians. Later, at the Hydaspes, Alexander seems to be aware of the advancing reinforcements and forces a decisive battle before they arrived; here at Pellium, Alexander shows no such awareness at all. This was likely a serious lack of scouting, but could equally be an indication that the wooded and mountainous terrain was extremely difficult terrain, directly resulting in the advancing enemy not being spotted by any scouts that Alexander had employed. I suspect that a combination of both can be blamed. We also see Alexander taking a dreadful and unnecessary risk with Philotas' foraging detachment: if it had been Alexander's intention to retreat, then he could have done so without delay by the deception device that he eventually chose; foraging was not required. This act seems to indicate that Alexander still intended to besiege the city, even though he was surrounded. These mistakes aside, Alexander's fighting withdrawal was masterful and controlled, and his tactic of withdrawing to a safe distance to trick the Illyrians into thinking he had left the region entirely was equally brilliant. Whilst Alexander essentially failed to capture the city, its destruction, along with the utter defeat of the Illyrian tribes, sent a message to others in the Balkans of the consequences of resistance to the new king. It is significant that Alexander never again throughout the whole of his career had any trouble from this historically-difficult and hostile region. Alexander's Balkan campaign as a whole clearly demonstrated the vast gulf that had developed between the military capabilities of the new Macedonia and her neighbours.

Any doubts that the siege of Pellium had raised about Alexander's abilities as a siege commander were to be quickly and completely erased by his capture of one of Greece's greatest cities: Thebes.

Thebes

Arrian provides us with the only full account of the outbreak of the Theban revolt; although Diodorus' account of the events of the siege are more detailed, and rather less favourable to Alexander.[52] Arrian tells us that a group of Theban citizens had allowed back into the city, under cover of night, a number of individuals that had been exiled by Philip after the Macedonian victory at Chaeronaea in 338.[53] These former exiles then murdered two members of the Macedonian garrison, named Amyntas and Timolaus. After this vicious act, they presented themselves to the assembly and incited the Thebans to revolt against the Macedonians by the apparently liberal use of such emotive words as 'liberty' and 'freedom'. They were further convinced that Alexander had in fact died during the Balkan campaign, as it had lasted for around four months, and no communication had been heard from the new king during that time. Demosthenes may also have produced a former Macedonian soldier who apparently swore to being an eye witness to Alexander's death. The assembly, perhaps against its better judgement, allowed itself to be swayed by the emotive language, and they began to lay siege to the Cadmea, which had held a Macedonian garrison since the allied Greek defeat at Chaeronea.

Arrian's story is entirely plausible; Philip did exile or execute large numbers of his Theban political enemies after Chaeronea, replacing them with a ruling body of 300 pro-Macedonian former exiles who had been invited back to their city.[54] The now-returning exiles were a necessary ingredient in order for the revolt to proceed; the first stages of the revolt are a virtual copy of the Theban revolt of 379.[55]

Once news of the events in Greece reached Alexander, he reacted in typical and decisive style. He immediately set off south through the passes of Eordaea and into Upper Macedonia, continuing south into the Haliacmon region and then on into Thessaly via the Peneus Valley. After seven days of forced marching he paused briefly at Pelinna, and then marched the remaining distance to Boeotia in a further five days.[56] The march to Thebes was conducted with terrifying speed; 390km in only thirteen days, one of which the army was resting. Thirty kilometres per day is an astonishing enough speed for an army in the ancient world to achieve, but when we consider the mountainous terrain that had to be traversed in order to reach Thebes in thirteen days, it is a truly staggering achievement. The need to reach Thebes at such speed was not overwhelming; the real reason for the march was that Alexander feared that the rebellion would spread to the rest of Greece. Alexander needed a show of force that would cow the other city-states into submission before they ever got to the point of revolt.

Alexander's arrival certainly caught the Thebans by surprise. He was at Onchestus, a three-hour march from Thebes, apparently before they even knew of his approach (and the city was under siege before the Athenians learnt he was south of Thermopylae); but they were certainly not unprepared. As soon as the oligarchic government set up by Philip had been overthrown, and the new democracy had voted for war, the Thebans had set about surrounding the Cadmea with deep trenches and heavy stockades so that neither reinforcements nor supply could reach the besieged Macedonian garrison.[57] The Thebans also sent an appeal for help to the Arcadians, Argives and Eleians, again no doubt citing Greek freedom as their rallying cry. The members of the Arcadian league even went so far as to organize a relief force, but ordered it to wait at the Isthmus of Corinth, assisting neither Thebes nor Macedon. There was also a minor rebellion in Elis where the pro-Macedonian faction was expelled and the government, presumably as well as its policy, was altered as a result.[58] We also know of a major debate in Athens where Demosthenes, a long-time opponent of Philip (and apparently now in receipt of Persian gold), along with Lycurgus, urged the demos to declare war on Alexander and send military aid to Thebes.[59] Athens did vote to support Thebes, but no troops were ever sent; in hindsight a very wise decision on the part of Athens given the ultimate fate of Thebes.

It would seem that Alexander's fear of the Theban revolt spreading to the rest of Greece was not without foundation. His lightning march was well timed; it had utterly destroyed any hope that there would be a united and widespread Greek revolt. All Alexander had to do was make a statement to the Greek world that Macedonia was still the superpower of Greece; all that had changed with the death of Philip was the name of the king.

Alexander arrived at Thebes to find his garrison hard pressed and surrounded by a double stockade, exactly the same device he was to use against the city of Sangala in India in 326. Alexander approached the city from the north and initially made camp there. The Thebans were certainly outnumbered by the Macedonians, but were in a strong defensive position, and to bolster their numbers they had enlisted slaves and metics to help man the walls.[60] Despite the potential for widespread resistance, Alexander was in a surprisingly-forgiving mood; he began the siege by offering the Thebans a 'period of grace, in case they should repent of their bad decisions and send an embassy to him'.[61] It is possible that Alexander reasoned that if the Thebans genuinely believed that he was dead, and given that he had no heir, then the League of Corinth treaty would be effectively nullified and thus their rising would be legally justified. It is far more likely, however, that Alexander was simply taking the opportunity to rest his troops and construct siege engines before the assault began. Given Alexander's need to send a message to the Greek world about resistance, a successful siege was a far more attractive and decisive outcome than a diplomatic resolution.

The former exiles realized that if they were to accept Alexander's terms, they would almost certainly be put to death and they argued in the assembly that the walls of Thebes were strong and that their hoplites and cavalry were the finest in Greece. They further argued that the Macedonian garrison on the Cadmea was isolated by troops inside Thebes, and by the newly-constructed double stockade around it. It seems likely that they also pointed out the possibility of a relief column from Athens or the Arcadian League, even though in reality both were unlikely. The former rebels evidently spoke persuasively and the assembly voted to reject Alexander's proposed terms.

The Thebans' answer to Alexander's offer of clemency was a sortie that was easily repulsed by the Macedonians.[62] Alexander then circled around the city and made camp to the south, opposite the Eleutherae Gate, at the closest point to the Cadmea, straddling the road to Athens. Given what had occurred at Pellium we might have expected Alexander to have been more cautious and keep friendly territory to his back rather than risking an attack from Thebes to the north and some other unspecified Greek force from the south. Throughout his career, however, Alexander can seldom be accused of caution. At Thebes he reasoned that the most advantageous strategic position was to camp as close to his garrison in the Cadmea as possible. The moving of Alexander's camp essentially changed the Macedonian posture, it was evident that they were preparing to attack against the most vulnerable section of the walls; yet still Alexander did not actually launch an attack. Arrian tells us that Alexander was still keen to win Theban friendship,[63] but this almost certainly comes from Ptolemy,[64] who made every effort to exonerate Alexander from any responsibility for the city's destruction. The reality of the situation is probably that Alexander was still resting his troops and constructing siege engines, given that a siege train could not possible have maintained his 30km-per-day rate of march from Pellium.

During the three-day delay before Alexander began the assault, the Thebans answered Alexander's continued offers of clemency by having a herald stand upon the battlements and proclaim that the Theban assembly would allow the commencement of negotiations once Alexander surrendered Antipater and Philotas to Thebes. The herald further proclaimed that 'all who wished to liberate Greece [were] to range themselves on their side'.[65] It is difficult to see exactly what the Thebans were attempting to achieve by the herald's message, but they only succeeded in enraging Alexander, with terrible consequences for their city-state.

The surviving sources differ as to exactly what occurred during the final assault upon the city, but it seems clear that Alexander had divided his forces and detached small units to various points around the city's perimeter. The Thebans had concentrated the finest of their troops on the double palisade between the Cadmea and the Macedonian camp, with the walls around the rest of the city being manned by slaves and metics.

Diodorus presents a picture of Alexander, at the sound of the *salpinx*, ordering a general assault to begin against the city. The Macedonians were almost irresistible, but the Thebans were apparently superior in strength and, with tremendous effort, held the Macedonians at bay. The battle wore on and Alexander saw that the Macedonians were becoming weary, perhaps not having fully recovered from the thirteen-day march from Pellium; at this point Alexander entered the fray with the hypaspists who had been held in reserve. The Thebans still fought on bravely, Alexander's presence not having the impact he expected. Alexander then noticed an unguarded postern gate and hurriedly detached Perdiccas and a large body of men to force an entry; this they did, and once they were inside the city the Theban resistance crumbled and the city was lost.[66]

Arrian's version, coming from Ptolemy, has a very different character. He tells us that Perdiccas and his *taxis* were camped close to the palisade and that he began the assault himself without waiting for orders from Alexander. Perhaps he had seen a glaring weakness in the defences of the palisade, perhaps he had received some form of signal from the defenders in the Cadmea, or perhaps this was the result of drunken revelling. Either way, Perdiccas quickly forced his way inside the palisade, but the defenders recovered rapidly and were in the process of cutting him off from the main camp. Upon seeing this, Amyntas joined the fray, closely followed by Alexander ordering a general assault. Perdiccas was wounded during the initial stages of the assault on the second palisade and took no further part in the siege. The troops of his *taxis* fought on, however, with support from Alexander and a unit of archers. The Theban defenders fought desperately for their survival and became boxed up on the 'sunken road which runs down by the Heracleum'. At the word of command, the Thebans stopped their retreat and turned to face the Macedonians and succeeded in driving them back some distance; during this action the commander of Alexander's Cretan archers, Eurybotas, was killed along with seventy of his men. Alexander countered with an infantry assault in close order; the rout gave way to panic and ultimately violent slaughter. The Theban last stand near the Ampheum was brave but futile. The terror that followed was, apparently, driven more by the traditional enemies of Thebes, the Phocians, Plataeans and men from various other Boeotian towns, than by the Macedonians.[67] In every account, Thebes was razed to the ground and the survivors sold into slavery.

Macedonian losses were significant: 500 dead. But Theban losses far worse: 7,000 dead and 30,000 sold into slavery. The sale brought much-needed revenue into the Macedonian treasury, some 440 talents; each Theban being worth on average 88 drachmae.[68]

The two versions both have the same end result, the destruction of Thebes, but occur along very different lines. Arrian, following Ptolemy, was clearly attempting to remove any blame for the city's destruction from Alexander; understandable given the sometimes apologetic nature of his history coupled with the revulsion that it caused in the rest of Greece. His account is not as anti-Perdiccas as some have argued however. Perdiccas and Ptolemy were later rivals and it is all to easy to put the blame upon Perdiccas' shoulders, but Arrian states quite clearly that Perdiccas was wounded during the assault on the second palisade and took no further part in the battle. He can, therefore, not be blamed for the atrocities that were committed later.[69] Arrian's account is so obviously apologetic, however, that I believe Diodorus to be the more reliable on this occasion. The siege began with Alexander ordering a general assault, and Perdiccas only broke through after receiving orders to attack an unguarded postern gate.

Historians have argued for centuries on the question of the destruction of Thebes, and what Alexander hoped to achieve. It can be argued that he desired to cause such fear amongst the southern Greek states that they would not dare to repeat the mistake of Thebes in openly rebelling against Macedonian control. Historians who would argue for this hypothesis would also likely argue that Alexander hoped that with one excessively-violent act he would prevent his being delayed in Greece by having to put down many minor rebellions. Alexander was certainly keen to continue the invasion of Persia that his father had tentatively begun in 336. It is true that the destruction of Thebes did cow the Greeks into cooperation for some years, and that the members of the League of Corinth generally ignored the revolt of Agis the Spartan in 331 (the Peloponnese was not part of the League and was therefore outside of Alexander's empire). It would also be true to argue that Alexander seemed desperately short of money during the early part of his reign, and the 440 talents were a very welcome boost to his empty coffers. The mistake usually made when considering the fate of Thebes, I believe, is to assume premeditation. It is a truism in the ancient world that 'to the victor goes the spoils'; after almost every city fell, women would have been brutalized, slaughter and looting would have been endemic and was almost impossible for any commander to stop, so it is not surprising that in that environment fires could be started as part of the general looting. The Macedonians were also taking out their frustrations on Thebes after a difficult Balkan campaign, and the failure to loot Pellium, followed by a difficult forced march into central Greece. This would have been magnified by the presence, as noted above, of a number of troops from cities that were traditionally the hated enemy of Thebes; decades of rivalry and repression would have also bubbled to the surface.

Whilst I would argue that the destruction of Thebes was probably accidental and not the result of policy on the part of Alexander, he may not have been altogether disappointed by the result. He got his psychological impact on the remaining Greek city states, received a much-needed cash injection (or perhaps 'fiscal stimulus' as we might say these days) whilst remaining relatively free of direct blame, essentially a win-win situation for the young king. Whilst the Greeks were cowed by the act, they certainly appeared to blame Alexander for the destruction of Thebes; the act, deliberate or otherwise, meant that Alexander would never be truly accepted by the Greeks, particularly the Athenians. He had proved himself to be a barbarian by perpetrating such an act, although I would note again that the Athenians did not join Agis' revolt in 331. The fear of a repeat of the fate of Thebes was still strong even five years after the event.

Alexander did not delay long in Greece after Thebes; he was impatient to begin his conquest of Persia. The great host gathered together in Macedonia and was divided between those who were part of the army of invasion, and those that were left behind with Antipater to garrison Greece and quell any rebellion. In terms of Macedonians, the numbers were close to identical; likely six *taxeis* of *Pezhetairoi* and three of hypaspists in each element, 12,000 Macedonian heavy infantry in total. Alexander probably also left behind 1,800 Companion Cavalry, the same number he took with him into Persia. The major part of the army of invasion that was different from the garrison of Greece was the allied contingent. Alexander took thousands of men from Thrace and the Balkans. This was a deliberate policy to reduce the numbers of young men in these regions and therefore to further reduce the likelihood of rebellion. This was a foreshadowing of the later Roman policy regarding their auxiliary legions.

The host set off east from Macedonia and marched through Thrace, probably picking up the remainder of his allied contingent *en route* to the Hellespont. Alexander crossed the Hellespont in 334 and threw a spear into the Asian side, claiming it to be 'spear-won territory', and was quickly joined by Parmenio and the remnants of the expeditionary force that Philip had sent to the region two years previously. Alexander was no doubt impatient for battle, and he did not have to wait long. The western Persian satraps commanding a force that was heavily reliant upon cavalry and mercenary infantry, commanded by Memnon of Rhodes, awaited Alexander on the banks of the Granicus River. This was Alexander's first major test, and he was not found wanting (see my forthcoming book, *The Field Campaigns of Alexander the Great*).

Chapter 3

Miletus and Halicarnassus: 334

Miletus

After the defeat of the western Persian satraps at the Granicus, Alexander moved south, down the western coast of Asia Minor. The Macedonians paused briefly at Ephesus, where Alexander made sacrifice to Artemis, before continuing south to Miletus. The city of Miletus was an ideal location for the Persians to use as a potential base of operations from which to launch a counter-attack on mainland Greece. It was surrounded on three sides by sea, jutting as it did into the Latmian gulf, and well fortified on the landward side. The ruins of the city are now in a rather different position, lying some 10km from the coast; this is due to the mouth of the Maeander River having silted up over the centuries. A portion of the army had been detached on a secondary mission of conquest, but Alexander still controlled the cream of the army of invasion: the *agema* of the Companion Cavalry, the Agrianians and archers, the Thracian cavalry and an unspecified number of heavy infantry *taxeis*.

Whilst Alexander was at Ephesus, the Persian commander of Miletus, a man called Hegisistratus, had offered to surrender to Alexander, and Alexander was no doubt expecting to receive the surrender of the city without incident, hence the relative lack of troops in his entourage. The presence of a Persian fleet of some 400 warships only three days away from his city filled Hegisistratus with renewed hope and a desire to resist; when Alexander arrived he found the gates of the city closed. Although Alexander expected the city to be surrendered to him without incident, he had anticipated the possibility of Hegisistratus' change of heart. His own fleet of 160 ships, commanded by Nicanor, had taken up a position just off Miletus on the island of Lade.[70] The island was fortified and garrisoned with 4,000 troops to further reduce the possibility of the Persians using it as a base of operations and safe anchorage.

With the inability of the Persians to land on the island of Lade, they were forced to make their anchorage off Mycale, some 15km south of Miletus. Naval battles in the ancient world only occurred, as with hoplite battles on land, when both sides were prepared to do battle, and there was little to no chance of Alexander offering an engagement for two reasons. Firstly, his own fleet was less than half the size of the Persian. Second, the Persian fleet, consisting of seasoned Phoenician and Cypriot warships, was far superior in quality. Alexander's fleet was reltively untrained; the Greek city-states had not sent their best ships and crews to serve him. Parmenio had, apparently, argued for a naval battle, but Alexander had rejected the idea, citing the untrained nature of his own fleet, and the potential impact on Greece if he were to be defeated. This is a rare instance of Parmenio proposing the ambitious strategy, and Alexander choosing caution as the safer option.

In lieu of naval operations, Alexander began the siege on land. The presence of his fleet off Lade meant that the defenders could not be supplied or reinforced by sea, and the city was easily blockaded by land, given the geography of the peninsula. The outer city had been abandoned by the defenders upon Alexander's approach, and was occupied without incident; the defenders had retired to the inner citadel that was smaller and more defensible.

After the occupation of the main city, Alexander received an embassy from a well respected Milesian citizen named Glaucippus. The offer was that the city, and notably its harbour, would become a free city; open to both Persian and Macedonian alike and be ruled by neither.[71] Alexander rejected the proposal out of hand, as he was to do in response to an identical offer from Tyre in 332 before the commencement of that siege. Alexander could not allow a port as important as Miletus to remain available to the Persians. Although he had not yet formalized his proposal of defeating the Persian navy on land, we can only assume that the embryonic idea for that strategy was already in his thoughts.

At dawn the following day, Alexander moved forward with his siege engines, which, in all probability, included stone-throwing catapults. We know that these new inventions were used at the siege of Halicarnassus, and I think it highly likely that they were also used here. If this is the case, then this was the first time in history of stone-throwing catapults being used against a fortification. The artillery pieces were used to clear away the defenders from the walls before the battering rams and scaling ladders were brought to bear. The walls were easily breached in several locations, and the city quickly fell. During these final operations, Alexander's Greek fleet formed a ring around the city. We are told that this was to prevent any possibility of the Persian fleet rendering assistance to the besieged city. Whilst this is likely, we should consider the possibility of ship-borne artillery also being deployed. Although there is no positive evidence for this, it is something that occurred during Tyre, and is a possibility here. Either way, the allied Greek fleet successfully prevented any assistance from the Persian's reaching Miletus.

Our sources give only a very foreshortened picture of the siege, essentially implying that it all took place in a single day. This seems unlikely, but it was certainly not a protracted siege operation. As the walls were breached, there was general panic amongst the civilian population who had no doubt heard of the fate of Thebes. They immediately offered to surrender to Alexander and begged for lenience, citing their resistance to Persian rule during the Ionian revolt. Our sources further carry no references to the fate of the Milesians once their city fell, or of Alexander's response to their pleas, but given that the city continued to exist after the siege, we can assume leniency on the part of Alexander. We do know, however, that the defenders, a body consisting entirely of Greek mercenaries, were slaughtered save for a small number who escaped. Alexander would have been all too quick to remind any who objected that it was strictly forbidden by the agreement of the League of Corinth for Greeks to take up arms against other Greeks. Alexander shows the same lack of sympathy as he did to the Greek mercenaries in Persian service after his victory at the Granicus.

Around 300 of the defenders did, however, escape the fall of the city by using their shields as makeshift rafts and 'sailing' to one of the many small rocky islets off Miletus (which Arrian notes as being unnamed).[72] Alexander made preparations to land on the islet by attaching scaling ladders to the fore of a number of his triremes with the intention of having marines scale the ladders and thereby gain a foothold on the rocky outcrop. The defenders, showing remarkable bravery, did not ask for terms but prepared to fight to the death. Alexander was so taken with their actions that he offered clemency, and employment within the army, which they readily accepted.

Alexander, having captured Miletus, had to force the Persian navy to withdraw, and do so without offering a naval battle. He achieved this by exploiting the fact that ancient triremes were too small to carry a great many supplies on board. Alexander sent Philotas with the Companion Cavalry and three *taxeis* of heavy infantry around the coast towards Mycale. Once there they acted to prevent the Persians from re-supplying their ships with the waters of the Maeander River; the Persians were left with no choice but to withdraw to the protection of the Athenian *cleruchs* on the island of Samos.

The siege of Miletus should have taught Alexander a valuable lesson: that a fleet could be extremely useful militarily, even if it did not offer battle to the Persian navy by being able to blockade a port. This is to say nothing, of course, of its ability to transport large numbers of troops quickly and to maintain lines of supply and communication with Macedonia. Even if these lessons had been apparent to Alexander, he appears to have ignored them as he now took the much debated decision to disband his fleet, save for a few Athenian vessels that were kept as much as hostages for the good behaviour of their mother city as for any other reason. The disbandment of the fleet is, strictly speaking, beyond the scope of a book on Alexander's sieges. However, I include an examination of the decision, as its direct effect was that Alexander needed to besiege and capture every Persian port between Miletus and Egypt; its relevance is, therefore, clear.

Arrian gives us five specific reasons for Alexander's decision to disband his Greek fleet:[73]

1. Lack of money.
2. The Persian navy was far superior in quality and strength to his own.
3. Alexander was unwilling to risk any losses, in ships or men, in a naval battle.
4. Alexander believed that he no longer needed a fleet as he was now 'master of the continent'.
5. He intended to defeat the Persian navy on land by depriving it of its ports.

Lack of money is the reason most commonly accepted by modern historians as the major factor in Alexander's decision; it is also one of only two reasons cited by Diodorus.[74] This conclusion is flawed for two reasons, though. Firstly, the fleet was supplied by the member states of the League of Corinth; it is therefore reasonable to assume – although we do not know this directly – that the cost of their upkeep would also fall on these states, and not on Alexander. The fleet would, effectively, have cost him almost nothing to maintain as the Macedonian element was small. Secondly, Alexander should not have been short of funds at this point in his career. Just a few months later at Gordium, during the winter of 334/3, Alexander invested 500 talents on raising a new fleet and 600 talents were allotted to pay for the upkeep of garrisons on the Greek mainland.[75] Alexander had no opportunity to significantly increase his resources between Miletus and Gordium, and therefore must have already had access to significant funds at the time of the fleet's disbandment.

On the second point, Arrian is correct to say that the Persian fleet was superior to Alexander's, both in numbers and quality. This is not a reason to demobilize the fleet, however, as this would leave the islands and the mainland defenceless and open to a counter-attack by the Persians, a strategy that was evidently considered by Memnon. It is fortunate indeed for Alexander that Memnon died so soon after the decision was made and that he was not able to carry out his plan. Further to the defence of Greece, Miletus had demonstrated to Alexander the usefulness of a fleet, even if he was not prepared to offer open battle. This evident lack of quality and numbers amongst Alexander's Greek fleet was more of an argument for increasing investment in the fleet, rather than ridding himself of it completely.

Points two and three are certainly linked: Alexander was unwilling to offer a naval battle because of the potential ramifications of any resulting defeat. If he had chosen a naval battle, his strategy would almost certainly have involved a heavy reliance on marines, most likely the hypaspists, and he could not afford to risk any losses amongst this contingent, as they were a vital component of every one of his land campaigns. The likelihood of Alexander fighting this sort of naval battle would be the result of his total lack of experience or knowledge of this form of warfare. The only occasions when Alexander ever used a navy was in support of his land operations, such as at Miletus and Tyre, or to assist in the crossing of a river, as with the Hydaspes.

Arrian's fourth point, that Alexander did not need a fleet, as he already controlled the whole continent, is extraordinary and demonstrably untrue. Even if we take Arrian to be referring to Asia Minor, rather than the whole of Asia, then it still was nowhere near true. It is hard to see why Arrian (or his source) would make such a claim.

This strategy of defeating the Persian navy on land is famous, and on the surface, fairly sound. In the ancient world, warships could not carry any great quantity of supplies and so had to dock at a friendly port every evening to re-supply with food and fresh water, and to allow the sailors the time and space to exercise and sleep. It is also true that this strategy ultimately worked; the Persian fleet did collapse as Alexander captured key cities on the Phoenician coast, but the strategy had at least two serious flaws. Firstly, a competent commander, as Memnon surely was, had a free hand to act as he wished in the Aegean, to overrun all of the islands and carry the fight to the mainland, where several states would more than likely have revolted given the opportunity. At the very least, the Persians could attack the coastal areas of Asia Minor and land troops in Alexander's rear, as they in fact did at Tenedos. Secondly, it does not take any account of the fact that a significant portion of the Persian fleet was from Cyprus, which would theoretically have been completely unaffected by Alexander's strategy. Although these ships would still have needed mainland ports in order to operate, they could have remained loyal to the Persians and able to harass Alexander's lines of supply and communication. Alexander essentially relied upon luck to overcome these two problems, which was uncharacteristic. His planning was usually far more meticulous than this and his strategies were well thought out; which leads me to conclude that his decision here was not a purely tactical or strategic one, but something else.

If the decision to disband the fleet was not taken on military grounds, nor was it forced upon him by lack of funds, or any of the other reasons Arrian gives, why did he make this decision? I suspect that the truth lies in something that Arrian comes close to mentioning, but does not specifically say. He points out that any loss in battle could lead to disaffection and potential rebellion in Greece. This raises the question of loyalty. The allied troops with the army were loyal to Alexander, although this could have been because of a fear of reprisals at home if they were not. They did have ample opportunities to be disloyal, including during the set-piece battles where they could have easily caused a defeat of Alexander by attacking the Macedonians' rear, rather than passively acting as his second line. It could also have been because of the presence of thousands of heavily-armed, battle-hardened Macedonians. The fleet, of course, would very quickly have been far away from the location of the king and the army, Alexander's personality and influence would have had far less of an impact on them, and the opportunity for disloyalty would have been exponentially greater the further Alexander progressed into Asia, and far easier to act upon. The fact that he retained the twenty Athenian vessels is an indication that he wanted to try to retain some specifically-Athenian hostages, but 160 potentially disloyal vessels was too great a risk.[76]

We should also note that Alexander in fact possessed two fleets, that of the League of Corinth, which was now disbanded, and that from Macedonia numbering sixty ships. There is no possibility of Alexander having dismissed all of his fleet as he needed to maintain control of the Hellespont to ensure his own lines of supply and communication with Macedonia, but also to keep open the corn route from the Black Sea, which was essential to the Greek states, and especially Athens.[77] Maintaining the corn routes for the city-states was essential in ensuring their continued loyalty. If they ever rebelled, Alexander could easily cut off their grain and starve them into submission, as long as he had a fleet in control of the Hellespont that is.

Halicarnassus

After the capture of Miletus, Alexander received news that Halicarnassus was preparing to resist under the guidance of Memnon of Rhodes, the man who Alexander had recently defeated at the Granicus. Memnon was apparently in command of a formidable force of native Persian troops and the remnants of the Greek mercenaries that had escaped after the Granicus. This potential resistance, coupled with the fact that it was the next closest port along the coast, and that it was the largest Persian port in the southwest Aegean, ensured that it was Alexander's next target.

Halicarnassus was in a naturally excellent defensive position; its walls were strongly fortified and ran along the edge of a small group of hills, adding to the city's defensive situation.[78] The outer circuit of the walls also contained three powerful citadels, rather than the more usual one; these were located at strategic points around the perimeter of the city. These citadels consisted of the original acropolis to the northwest, the fortification at the harbour entrance to the southwest, Salmacis, and the island stronghold of Zephyrium, the location of the tomb of Mausolus, one of the seven wonders of the ancient world. The fortress was also surrounded by a moat some 13m deep and 7m wide.[79] The defenders were further encouraged, and their position strengthened by, the presence of the Persian fleet, who now had no potential opponent to occupy their attentions. The defenders could be re-supplied and reinforced at will; the disbandment of the fleet meant that the siege would now be considerably more difficult, and would have to be conducted entirely on land. When Alexander arrived before the walls of the city in the autumn of 334, he no doubt expected a lengthy siege.

Memnon had only received news of his promotion the day before Alexander arrived, and he wasted no time in using his new authority. He first ordered a screen of ships to blockade the harbour, an unnecessary precaution given Alexander's lack of a fleet. He also gathered together all of the mercenaries who had been evacuated from the various cities in Alexander's path that surrendered without resistance. His final act was to carry out some emergency repair work to the already formidable defences.

Alexander approached the city from the northeast and made camp around 1km from the Mylasa gate. This was the sector that would bear the brunt of the Alexander's siege operations. The first day of the siege was something of a victory for the defenders, and is illustrative of Memnon's tactics. The Macedonians had, apparently, approached too close to the walls; Memnon immediately saw an opportunity to strike the first blow. He launched a sortie,

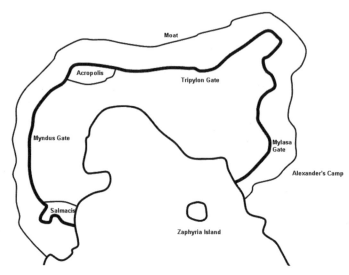

Figure 1: Sketch of the Siege of Halicarnassus

largely using missile troops to allow them the opportunity of getting back within the cities walls as soon as the Macedonians were able to organize their own counter-attack.

Several days later, Alexander took a substantial force consisting of the hypaspists, Companion Cavalry, the heavy infantry *taxeis* of Amyntas, Perdiccas and Meleager, along with the Agrianians and archers, to the west of the city with the intention of determining if the walls in that sector were weaker, and weather an assault in that sector would likely prove more profitable. Alexander apparently also hoped to capture Myndus, a city on the western end of the Halicarnassus peninsula, possession of which would have made the siege of Halicarnassus less problematic. Dissidents within the city had previously made contact with Alexander and offered to open the city gates if he came under cover of darkness. Alexander approached the city at around midnight according to Arrian, but the gates remained closed; the rebels had evidently been discovered and their plan foiled. Despite being utterly unprepared for a siege, possessing neither artillery, rams nor scaling ladders, Alexander ordered sapping operations to commence against the city and he succeeded in bringing down one of the city forts. This use of sapping is the first time in Alexander's career that he attempted such a device, and it proved partially successful, with the collapse of the tower. The fall of the fort did not, however, compromise the integrity of the defensive wall, and the defenders were soon reinforced by mercenaries arriving by sea from Halicarnassus. Alexander was forced, no doubt with a considerable degree of frustration, to abandon the attempted siege.[80]

It seems that the Macedonians made a number of unsuccessful, and probably rather half-hearted, attempts to capture Halicarnassus without the benefits of siege equipment. It was painfully apparent to Alexander that without artillery pieces, the fortress was simply too strong to be stormed. In order to bring his siege train from Miletus to Halicarnassus as quickly as possible, Alexander took a tremendous risk: he had his siege engines loaded onto the remaining ships that were not disbanded and sailed from Miletus to Halicarnassus, where they were unloaded and moved into position without incident. This is a quite remarkable statement about ancient navies. The Persians had a force of 400 warships stationed in and around the harbour of Halicarnassus, and yet the Athenian vessels, whose crews we know were of dubious quality, were still able to evade the Persians and land their cargo. They were also, evidently, able to leave the vicinity of the city without incident. It is difficult to defend Alexander's risk on this point, Miletus was very close to Halicarnassus, and the land route was in Alexander's hands. Why take the risk of losing, either in battle or betrayal, the Athenian hostages along with his siege train? This decision is of little tactical value and was an unnecessary risk by the young king.

The arrival of the siege engines filled the Macedonians with renewed vigour, and they set about filling the northern and eastern sections of the moat, so as to allow the close approach of rams and towers, as well as direct assault from scaling ladders. Arrian tells us that the moat was filled in without incident, and the towers were brought into a position from which the assault proper would begin the following day. During the night, Memnon again tried to gain the initiative in the siege by launching a daring night time sortie in an attempt to burn the siege engines and towers that it was apparent were about to bombard the walls. Once these men were engaged, the noise of the encounter, amplified by the fact it was night, drew the attention of the men of the hypaspists corps, who drove the attackers back with relative ease. Memnon suffered some 170 casualties during the attempt, with Alexander losing only 16 killed and 300 wounded. Arrian tells us that the disproportionately high number of wounded troops was due to the encounter taking place in the dark 'when it is more difficult to defend oneself'.[81]

After this encounter, the defenders busied themselves in continuing to strengthen the defences, whilst the besiegers made ever more siege engines in preparation for the start of the direct assault against the walls. Arrian tells us that a few days after Memnon's sortie, although in reality it could well have been a couple of weeks, two drunken soldiers from Perdiccas' *taxis* advanced alone towards the walls in a drunken attempt to prove who was the braver.[82] They evidently made a number of approaches to the walls, but always stayed out of missile range. As time went on, however, perhaps under the influence of ever greater quantities of un-watered wine, they picked up their weapons and attacked the wall on the high ground facing Mylasa. Arrian tells us that they had no intention of actually forcing a fight, simply intending to show 'what mighty fellows they were'. The defenders watched the Macedonians for a while as they repeatedly approached the walls whilst unarmed, but not close enough to allow the defenders to fire upon them. As soon as the Macedonians took up their weapons and attacked the walls, Memnon sortied against them with a far larger body of men. These two foolish Macedonians were quickly killed, but Memnon's men did not retreat into the safety of the city. They started to fire missile weapons against the Macedonians in their camp, safe in the belief that they were on higher ground and close enough to the gates to run for safety if required. The attack against the camp prompted the Macedonians to rally and launch their own attack against Memnon's position.

The initial Macedonian response was similar to that of Memnon, to maintain a distance and hurl missiles at the attackers. This act of not rushing into the assault after seeing two fellow Macedonians killed is illustrative of the discipline of the Macedonian heavy infantry, although the very fact of the two attacking the walls individually tells us that this discipline was neither iron-clad nor was it universal, especially when wine was involved. Arrian tells us that the Halicarnasians who came too close to the Macedonians were quickly killed, suggesting that they were not as disciplined as the Macedonians in staying out of missile range.[83]

The position that Memnon had taken up gave them a significant tactical advantage: they were on higher ground, which meant that their missile weapons could effectively travel slightly further, whilst at the same time being in an advantageous position if any direct attack came.

More Macedonians of Perdiccas' *taxis* formed up behind those hurling missiles, and at the same time more of the Halicarnassians joined those on high ground outside of the city. The walls facing the Macedonian camp should also have been well stocked with defenders, but apparently this was not the case; evidently most of the available manpower in that sector of the city had been requisitioned to take part in the sortie. This lack of defenders was not immediately significant, but it was to be the cause of the city almost falling to

Alexander as the forward troops fell back to the city after a brief skirmish. The Halicarnassians outnumbered the Macedonians immediately outside the walls, again indicating that this was a major commitment of men by Memnon. What had started as a boasting contest between two drunken Macedonians, very quickly escalated into a major engagement for both sides.

When the Macedonians were sufficiently organized, they attacked the Halicarnassians on the hill and quickly drove them back, despite the tactical disadvantage that the hill represented. The Halicarnassians were quickly driven back within the gates of the city, and the gates were only just closed in time to prevent the Macedonians gaining access, and the city potentially falling. Some of the defenders may well have been stranded outside of the city, as it seems unlikely that all of them could have got to safety before the gates were closed. The fact that so many of the defenders had been committed to the sortie, leaving the walls denuded of defenders, was critical at this point; they were simply unable to drive the Macedonians back with a hail of missiles from above as should have been the case. The lack of rams and ladders meant it was difficult for the Macedonians to continue the assault directly, and the defenders would have gradually manned the walls and towers that were in good repair as they made the safety of the city, and then climbed the walls. Finally, after much effort, the Macedonians were driven back.

Arrian tells us that the collapse of two towers and the intervening stretch of wall would have offered an easy entrance to the Macedonians if they had attacked in force. This statement needs further examination, however.[84] Alexander had not yet been attacking the walls directly with his siege equipment, and therefore had not brought down the walls previously. Indeed, we know that he had spent several days constructing new siege engines and those from Miletus had only recently arrived by sea. We can also presume that the skirmish that resulted from the drunken boasting would not have been supported by siege engines, catapults, rams or siege towers: the response was too rapid to allow for a general assault to be organized. The only conclusion is, therefore, that the walls of the city were in a very poor condition when Alexander arrived outside of the walls. This is why we hear of the defenders frantically constructing defensive fortifications when the Macedonians were building their own siege engines. The defenders must have worked tirelessly as the Macedonians approached to build a curtain wall that was of sufficient strength to deter the Macedonians from making an initial assault in strength against that sector as soon as they arrived. The general state of the walls in that sector is a further reason that Alexander chose to concentrate his assault against the east and northeast of the city.

When the Macedonians had been driven back, and as dawn began to break, it became apparent to Alexander that there had been some significant loss of life amongst his Macedonians. Diodorus tells us that he was forced to make a formal request for a cease fire in order to recover the dead so they could be given a proper burial. If true, this would not have been a unique event in Alexander's career, but it would have been extremely rare, and there seems no obvious motive for invention. Diodorus presented the whole incident as an unqualified defeat. Arrian evidently attempted to put a positive spin on the matter by noting that the city almost fell, but glosses over the fact that the assault was the result of undisciplined drunkenness and of individuals not obeying orders, and was a failure at best, an expensive embarrassment at worst.[85]

The drunken attack occurred the night before Alexander was ready to launch his main assault against the walls, but the incident would have caused some delay as he recovered his dead and performed the proper burial rituals. After that, Alexander made his final preparations, and the siege engines were brought to bear against the newly-constructed curtain wall. As the siege towers were being dragged, or pushed, into position, the defenders once again sallied forth from the city. The defenders' attack was two-pronged: the first division was against the sector where Alexander was taking personal command near the curtain wall; the other attack was launched later from the Tripylon Gate to the north of the city, a sector from which the Macedonians did not expect an attack.[86] This two-pronged attack was a sophisticated and well-thought-out stratagem by Memnon and Ephialtes, and had clearly been well planned in advance. It would have been impossible to have organized such a coordinated attack only upon seeing the siege towers being brought forward. This implies that Memnon had probably devised a number of defensive strategies that were ready to be used as the opportunity presented itself.

Alexander's troops quickly drove the attackers back towards the walls, but this was exactly Ephialtes' plan. In a strategy reminiscent of Miltiades at Marathon, Ephialtes kept his own group of men back from the fighting, and once the first wave had retreated far enough, drawing the Macedonians inwards, he counter-attacked from the Tripylon Gate against the advancing Macedonians. The Macedonians found themselves under attack on three sides, as well as from missile weapons thrown from the battlements above. Alexander had allowed himself to be drawn into a very difficult position; he had evidently believed that the fall of the city was underway, as at Thebes the previous year, but Memnon and Ephialtes were excellent tacticians. Alexander had led the assault with the younger men of the *pezhetairoi*, Philip's long-serving veterans being held in reserve; it was this decision that saved many Macedonian lives. When the veteran troops saw the evolving situation, they readied themselves and advanced upon the enemy, quickly turning the tide of the encounter back in the Macedonians' favour.

The objective of this sortie was the destruction of Alexander's siege towers. The defenders knew that these could easily be used to allow large numbers of attackers to pepper the defenders with missile fire, denuding the walls before they were breached. The sortie was led by Ephialtes, and the men carried burning torches that they hurled at the wooden siege towers. One of the towers quickly caught fire and was destroyed, but Alexander rallied the men under his immediate command and drove the Halicarnassians back within the city in time to save the second tower. As well as the use of infantry to drive back the defenders, 'catapults mounted on towers kept up a continuous pressure by hurling heavy stones'. This is the first attested use in history of stone-throwing catapults being used during a siege; although they are used against infantry here, there is no reason to assume that they would not also have been used against the walls, as at Tyre.[87]

The sortie of Ephialtes was a partial success: one of the towers had been destroyed, but the threat that they presented had not been removed. The second attack from the Tripylon Gate was far less successful: they were met by Ptolemy (captain of the royal guard) and probably the hypaspists, along with a detachment of light infantry. The attackers were quickly beaten back with disastrous consequences: they all fled across a bridge over the dyke that surrounded the city, which collapsed under the collective weight. Many died as they fell into the dyke, and many more were killed by missiles thrown by the Macedonians as the Halicarnassians attempted to scramble to safety. The attackers, now in a desperate situation, were doomed when the city gates were closed too soon, for fear that the Macedonians might break into the city. The slaughter that occurred outside of the gates was terrible, and would have been devastating on the morale of the defenders as they could do little more than simply watch their friends being cut down. Memnon lost around 1,000 men (including Ephialtes himself) in these sorties; overall it was a risky gamble that failed in its objective of preventing the siege towers from reaching the walls of the city, and cost the defenders many men that they could ill afford to lose.

Following Ephialtes' death and the relative failure of the final sortie, Memnon and the Persian commander, Orontobates, came to the decision that the city could not be held for much longer against the Macedonians, especially now that their siege engines were operational and constantly guarded. Parts of the walls had collapsed, other sections were close to collapse and the defenders had lost many men in combat. Around midnight, they set fire to the magazines in the city, the houses closest to the walls and the wooden tower that had been constructed to help the defence of the city. Once the fires were set, the wind took over and the conflagration spread to the rest of the city, much of which was soon alight. The surviving forces withdrew to the island stronghold of Salmacis, probably the citadel of Arconnesus (Kara Ada) just off the coast of Halicarnassus and technically still part of the city.

Alexander evidently did not want the city razed to the ground and quickly breached the walls giving orders to his men to kill anyone they saw setting fires, while townspeople were to be rescued from the flames.[88] If true, this shows that the Macedonians were capable of resisting the urge to loot and pillage at the end of a siege. It further suggests that the destruction of Thebes was more the result of frustration and of long-standing scores being settled, than of any lack of discipline.

Once day broke, Alexander could see the level of destruction in the city, and the fact that the island fortress was heavily defended by Memnon and his surviving mercenaries. Seeing that any siege of the island would be both time consuming and costly in terms of the potential loss of Macedonian life, he decided to leave a detachment of troops to continue the siege. Alexander decided to continue the conquest of Persia by marching first east along the coast, and then inland towards Gordium and ultimately towards Cilicia and the campaign of Issus. The continued siege would have been costly, but this can not be the reason for abandoning it. After all, Ptolemy was left behind to conduct the siege and, therefore, the losses were going to occur whether they were commanded by Alexander or Ptolemy. Alexander's main reasons for abandoning the siege were twofold. Firstly, he needed to continue with his strategy of defeating the Persian navy on land. The sooner he was able to achieve this, the sooner he would secure the Macedonian homeland, as well as the wider Greek world, from a Memnon-led counter-attack. The Persian fleet would not have been able to use the island fortress for supply indefinitely as it would have very limited supplies itself. The fleet would have been required to keep the island supplied, not vice-versa. Alexander, therefore, could legitimately claim to have deprived the Persians of their major port in southwest Asia Minor before moving on. Alexander's second main reason for leaving Halicarnassus before its final fall was simply impatience; he had been delayed for longer than he would have wished at Halicarnassus, and the prospect of a further delay of probably months at least would have been intolerable. Alexander was keen to engage in battle with Darius, and he could only achieve this by moving further east as soon as possible.

There are two separate accounts of Halicarnassus, those of Diodorus and Arrian. Diodorus certainly presents this campaign as the least impressive of Alexander's career, although Arrian is less negative. Even in Arrian, however, Halicarnassus is far from an overwhelming success; still we find the undisciplined soldiers of Perdiccas' *taxis* and still we find Alexander being taken by surprise by Ephialtes' sortie, as well as the lack of protection for his siege engines and towers. Innovation throughout the whole siege was typically as a reaction to the actions of Memnon and Ephialtes in both traditions.[89] Whilst it is true that he was, to a point, successful, he only captured part of the city and did not deprive the Persian navy of its base; that was ultimately left to Ptolemy.

In contrast to Alexander's shortcomings, Memnon and Ephialtes showed themselves to be commanders of the highest order. Memnon successfully sealed breaches in the walls where they occurred, he constructed a huge tower from which to shower the attackers with missiles and he conducted a series of sorties that always had Alexander on the back foot whilst Ephialtes led the first sortie with distinction.

With hindsight, Alexander was certainly successful in the capture of Halicarnassus, and it did not take too long, for which he should be given credit. We can also say that he learned tough lessons from his mistakes here that he was to put into practice during later sieges (i.e. Tyre and Gaza). We can add that Alexander was certainly lucky that Memnon died when he did.

Chapter 4
Tyre: 332

From Gordium Alexander marched towards the region of Cilicia where he was ultimately to meet Darius for the first time, and convincingly defeat the Persian host with a brilliant series of flanking attacks. After Darius had fled the field, Alexander was faced with a significant strategic decision: chase Darius and force a final resolution, or continue south down the Phoenician coast and complete the capture of the Persian naval bases. To pursue Darius would be to leave the major Persian strongholds of Phoenicia and Egypt unconquered, as well as leaving the still-powerful and active Persian fleet with bases from which to operate and potentially take the war to the Greek mainland, as had been Memnon's strategy the previous year. The decision appears not to have been a difficult one for Alexander. He immediately set off south along the Phoenician coast towards Tyre, and ultimately Egypt. We also have to realize that for a man raised in the Greek world it would have been natural for him to wish to complete the conquest of the Mediterranean basin before moving further into the Persian heartlands. The decision left Darius free to move into the heartland of Persia and gather a new army, but Alexander reasoned that as he had defeated the Great King once, he could do it again.

Most of the coastal cities in Alexander's path south from Cilicia, such as Byblos and Sidon, surrendered without a struggle; the citizenry were evidently rather enthusiastic about the Macedonian conqueror. At Sidon, the king, Stratton II, a friend of Darius, was deposed by his people so that they could accept Alexander's terms peacefully. Tyre was to prove to be a far more reluctant addition to the growing Macedonian empire.[90] Before the siege began, Alexander was presented with the opportunity of preventing bloodshed by a delegation offering terms. On the way to Tyre, Alexander was met by representatives from the island city offering peaceful terms that would have allowed the Macedonians, Persians and Tyrians to co-exist. Curtius presents the Tyrians as more willing to accept an alliance with Alexander than subjugation to the Macedonians, which is supported by later events.[91] Alexander, perhaps realizing the strength of the Tyrian position, did not consider the offer for long, and gave an initially-positive response; he thanked them for their offer and informed them of his intention to make sacrifice in the temple of Heracles within the city.[92] The timing of Alexander's arrival at Tyre was unfortunate; his request for sacrifice coincided perfectly with the Tyrian festival of Melqart in February 332. Allowing Alexander to sacrifice in the temple at this time would have been tantamount to recognizing Alexander as king in the eyes of the citizens, and this they found impossible to accept. The Tyrian response was a refusal to permit any Persian or Macedonian entry to the city, and offered Alexander the opportunity to use the temple of Heracles in Old Tyre, on the mainland. Alexander's anger at this refusal by the citizens of Tyre is reported by both Arrian and Curtius, with the latter reporting it as more of an irrational temper tantrum.[93] It is possible that Alexander anticipated the Tyrian response, or at the very least used it to his advantage as a pretext to storm the city, although Alexander seldom felt the need to act only once a pretext had been found. Curtius is by far the most plausible source in describing the Tyrian reliance upon their defensive fortifications as their primary motive for resisting Alexander; they simply would not have imagined that Alexander would even have contemplated a siege of the island, especially with the still-active Persian fleet in the eastern Aegean. Diodorus on the other hand saw it as part of a grand strategy from the Persians to resist Alexander. This seems unlikely to say the least.

The question of weather Alexander needed to besiege and ultimately capture the city is an interesting one. It can be argued that Tyre could have been isolated by the Macedonians by the capture of every other port on the coast, and by the presence of a permanent garrison in Old Tyre to prevent them gaining access to the mainland. This would have resulted in the fortress being a true island surrounded by the growing Macedonian empire. If this had occurred, there is no reason that the Tyrians could not have held out indefinitely, as long as the Persians maintained control of the larger islands such as Crete and Rhodes. Even if Tyre were to have come over to Alexander voluntarily after some years of isolation, the potential to cause trouble in Greece could not be tolerated, nor could the challenge to Alexander's authority that the Tyrians had inadvertently made.[94] Alexander's thinking regarding the prospective siege is summed up in a speech in Arrian delivered to the Companions and other officers before the siege began:[95]

> Friends and fellow soldiers, I do not see how we can safely advance upon
> Egypt, so long as Persia controls the sea; and to pursue Darius with the

neutral city of Tyre in our rear and Egypt and Cyprus still in enemy hands would be a serious risk, especially in view of the situation in Greece. With our army on the track of Darius, far inland in the direction of Babylon, the Persians might well regain control of the coast, and thus be enabled with more power behind them to transfer the war to Greece, where Sparta is already openly hostile to us, and Athens, at the moment, is but an unwilling ally; fear, not friendliness, keeping her on our side. But with Tyre destroyed, all Phoenicia would be ours, and the Phoenician fleet, which both in numbers and quality is the predominant element in the sea-power of Persia, would very likely come over to us. The Phoenician seamen, ships' crews or fighting men, once their towns are in our hands, will hardly endure to face the perils of service at sea for the sake of others. The next step will be Cyprus: it will either join us without trouble on our part, or be easily taken by assault; then, with the accession of Cyprus and the united fleets of Macedon and Phoenicia, our supremacy at sea would be guaranteed, and the expedition to Egypt would thus be a simple matter, and finally, with Egypt in our hands we shall have no further cause for uneasiness about Greece: we shall be able to march on Babylon with security at home, with enhanced prestige, and with Persia excluded not only from the sea, but from the whole continent up to the Euphrates.

The island city of Tyre was, from the strategic standpoint, superbly sited. Its capture would prove to be the most difficult and challenging campaign of Alexander's entire career. The island was separated from the mainland by a strait four stades wide, of the order of 750m. Curtius also tells us that it was particularly exposed to southwesterly winds, a fact that would prove to be extremely important in the construction of the mole. Curtius states that it was this wind, and the waves it generated, that was the greatest obstacle to the construction of the mole. The strait was relatively shallow, until a couple of hundred metres from the fortress; at that point the sea bed fell away quite dramatically where the water reached three fathoms deep.[96] Tyrian confidence was further boosted by a delegation from Carthage who promised help against the Macedonians, help that in reality never materialized.

Curtius goes on to describe the quite-formidable Tyrian defences: catapults lining the walls, *harpagones* constructed to use against Alexander's siege engines, along with 'ravens' and other defensive siege devices. *Harpagones* were grappling irons, originally invented by Pericles; they are known to have been used by Alcibiades, and Livy describes their use by the Carthaginian navy. They were therefore something new to Alexander, but certainly not new to Greek warfare. The corvus (Greek *korax*) or raven (perhaps crow) was not the complex grappling hook and boarding bridge made famous by Duilius in the First Punic War, and described by Polyaenus. Curtius is imagining a simple grappling hook of the type used at Mycale in 36.[97] From both the perspectives of geography and defensive armaments, Tyre was extremely well situated to resist any proposed siege by Alexander, and could be re-supplied at will with food, water and fresh troops from the sea by the Persian fleet.

As a supreme tactician, Alexander would have considered all the options available to him; ultimately he came to the conclusion that leaving Tyre independent was an unacceptable risk. The only thing that remained to be considered was how to capture the city. The capture of fortified cities in the ancient world was difficult to say the least; the advantage always had been with the defenders behind their walls. In the case of Tyre, it was one of the richest cities in the Mediterranean and could easily be re-supplied. It also had a population probably in excess of 40,000 and thus was not short of men to defend the walls if necessary. Alexander would have been aware of his father's failed attempts to capture Perinthus and Byzantium; on both occasions the Macedonians were in a better position than at Tyre given that both were on land, and Philip was in possession of a fleet. He would also have known of the failed siege lasting thirteen years by the Babylonian King Nebuchadnezzar in the sixth century. A besieging army before the career of Alexander would typically have to rely upon treachery or starvation to capture a city, unless the walls were so weak they could be easily breached. A city with reasonable and well-kept defences was virtually impregnable. Tyre had almost every advantage that defenders in the ancient world could hope for, yet still Alexander resolved to besiege the fortress.

Alexander did have the advantage of stone throwing-catapults that Philip and earlier Greeks did not, but Tyre was too far offshore for them to reach the walls, so they were essentially useless from the land. If Alexander wanted to capture the city he had the two choices of treachery or force. His clumsy attempt at diplomacy had not worked, and treachery seemed unlikely, particularly given that there was no need for anyone within the city to feel threatened enough to try and save themselves by metaphorically, or actually, opening the gates to the conqueror. There was only one option: the city would have to be taken by force. The only way to do that was to directly engage the walls, and this line of reasoning lead Alexander unavoidably to the construction of the mole, one of the more celebrated military acts of his career. Once the decision to storm the fortress had been made, operations began almost immediately.

The siege of Tyre can be divided into two operational phases, the first of which began with the construction of the mole and ended with its destruction. The second was the construction of a much larger mole and the two giant siege towers, and eventually resulted in the fall of the city.

The first phase of the siege began with a tremendously symbolic act by Alexander: he apparently filled a wicker basket with rubble, carried it to the shore opposite Tyre and dropped it into the sea. Alexander himself had begun the construction of the mole. This act is reminiscent of Alexander standing at the prow of the first ship to cross the Hellespont and throwing a spear into the beach claiming Asia as 'spear-won territory', and is also reminiscent of dignitaries today laying the first foundation stone to symbolize the beginning of a major construction project. Alexander's act was no different.[98]

The mole itself was intended to be essentially a causeway from the mainland to the island, a means of directly engaging the city walls and enabling a slightly more traditional siege. It is a sobering thought that the final breakthrough of the walls did not come from the sector where the mole was being constructed, but it is certainly a mistake to say that the mole was unnecessary; it enabled Alexander to attack from various directions simultaneously as was his favoured strategy. More on this later.

For the construction of the mole to proceed without interruption, vast quantities of raw materials were required. Considerable numbers of trees must have been felled in nearby Lebanon, and the city of Old Tyre on the mainland facing the island was completely destroyed to provide the rubble required for the mole.[99] Considerable numbers of men were also required. We do not know their origins, but the only workers referred to in the sources are soldiers of the army. These were the ones who were attacked by the Tyrians onboard their ships. The construction workers likely were not all soldiers, however. The most menial tasks (felling trees, fetching water, etc.) were probably performed by local villagers, but of these people we hear nothing, nor do we know if they were paid or press-ganged into service. It is not surprising that the sources do not mention these people, if indeed they existed at all. Ancient writers almost never mention the lowest rungs of society, and at Tyre there were far more exciting and interesting things to write about than the local peasantry.

The construction process was quite simple, and it is perhaps surprising that the mole has survived to the present day. Alexander's mole is the only reason that the city of Tyre is now no longer an island, but is still connected to the mainland by that mole, now greatly silted up along its northern shore. Boulders of various sizes were physically carried from the ruins of Old Tyre and dropped into the water where they formed a more solid foundation than the sand and mud of the sea bed. The trees that had been felled and transported to the coast were cut into the shape of huge stakes that were driven into the sea bed on either side of what Alexander wanted to be the causeway. These would have the effect of holding the boulders in position and resisting the surging tides that ran down the coast. On top of the boulders was dropped sand which would fall between the larger rocks and provide stability, otherwise the weight of the catapults and siege towers that would ultimately be dragged along the mole would cause it to become dangerously unstable. As the mole began to rise above the level of the waves, a layer of earth was added, and then compacted, to add further stability as well as a platform from which to conduct operations. The mole was a tremendous engineering undertaking and it is a testimony to the ability of Alexander's engineers that it was initiated quickly with little or no planning; they simply knew what had to be done and started work.

The accounts of the siege are somewhat truncated; the actual construction of the mole seems to take place very rapidly when, in reality, it took months to get anywhere near the city. The first part of the construction work probably did proceed relatively quickly, however, as the water was shallow and the logistical problems were less acute given the proximity to the coast and the resources of Old Tyre. At first the Tyrians considered Alexander's attempts to be comical and indicative of extreme hubris; to attempt to capture an island by effectively taming the ocean and joining it to the land was considered preposterous. As progress was rapid during the early construction phase, the Tyrian response quickly changed.

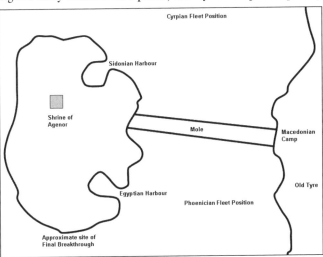

Figure 2: Sketch of the Siege of Tyre

The first phase proceeded relatively quickly and Alexander would no doubt have been greatly encouraged, but the mole soon hit deeper water; something like a third of the way to the island the sea bed drops away rapidly to a depth of around 5.5m. The Macedonians continued to drop boulders into the sea, but they had little effect, it would have looked as though the sea was simply swallowing them whole. Alexander was not a man who easily gave in when faced with a difficult situation, and with the same kind of determination that allowed him to believe that constructing a mole was the best course of action, he simply continued pouring stone and rocks into the sea. Eventually, and very slowly, the mole proceeded towards the island again.

The Tyrians probably began to get worried at around this time; they would have been well aware that the ocean floor dropped away rapidly as the island was neared, and they would have seen this as yet another line of defence against this novel form of attack, but seeing the mole continue its inexorable approach to the walls would have forced them to act more proactively. Once the mole, and therefore the workers, came within range of projectile weapons fired from the city walls, the construction teams came under constant attack, both from archers and defensive weaponry upon the walls and from seaborne raids at various points along the mole, led by marines based on board ships.[100]

These naval raids were in the form of missile troops, specifically archers and slingers, perhaps along with small arrow-firing artillery. The triremes that they were aboard sailed up and down the growing mole with impunity, attacking wherever there were vulnerable workers. The construction crews were almost completely defenceless; they were unarmed and there seemingly were few troops stationed on the mole to protect them from such an attack. It is curious that Alexander did not anticipate a sortie from the defenders as he had experienced several at Halicarnassus, and the defensive measures taken with the siege towers (hide coverings for example) clearly indicate that the previous siege was uppermost in his mind. Often during Alexander's career, he would use a small body of men to lure out the defenders onto ground of his choosing, and if Alexander had possessed a fleet, or had laid some kind of trap, then we may have speculated that this was what occurred at Tyre, but he did not. He must have anticipated the Tyrians using ships to attack the mole, and yet he did nothing to counter the threat immediately; this has to be considered a tactical mistake by Alexander.

Attacks from men aboard ship were almost impossible for Alexander to counter. His men on the mole were sitting ducks for the ship-borne archers, the casualties inflicted may not have been severe (it seems that ancient archers were far less effective than their counterparts carrying longbows of the later medieval period), but the effect upon morale, as well as on the progress of the mole, would have been severe.

After the first naval sortie by the defenders, consisting of marines onboard eight triremes, Alexander responded by diverting construction workers on the mole onto the creation of a series of portable wooden palisades along both sides of the mole to offer some protection from ship-borne missile fire, along with the construction of two siege towers at the end, to reign down missile fire of their own onto any naval vessels that strayed too close.

These two siege towers were impressive engineering feats in themselves, but are usually overlooked as they were on the mole, which was a far greater achievement. They were intended to be of a considerable height, so that missiles could rain down upon the Tyrians, thus preventing them from constantly attacking the construction workers.[101] This kind of suppressive fire is something we saw to cover the retreat before the Battle of Pellium, and is an example of something we see repeatedly during Alexander's career: the recycling of successful strategies.

During the siege of Halicarnassus, Alexander had spent considerable resources building siege engines, only to see some of them destroyed by fire during an audacious sortie by the defenders. Alexander was evidently a man who, sometimes at least, learned from previous mistakes, and at Tyre he took steps to protect the siege towers by draping skins and hides all over the exposed wooden surfaces, essentially in order to add a flame resistant covering.[102]

If, as noted earlier, the idea of a mole originated with the siege of Motya, then the idea of protecting the workers with siege engines would no doubt have come from the same siege.[103] The surprising thing is that it did not occur to Alexander to protect the mole and the workers in some way, long before he suffered serious casualties. This reactive nature of Alexander is confirmed by both Arrian and Curtius who make it clear that the towers were there for the defence of the mole.[104] They should also not be confused with the towers that were used to assault the walls later in the siege, these were two of the tallest siege towers ever constructed in the ancient world; the earlier ones on the mole were on a rather lesser scale.[105] If Alexander had taken the time to protect the workers properly, this would have slowed the progress of the construction of the mole. What we see is a mistake on the part of Alexander, one caused by his impatience and carelessness, as the siege was already several months old, and he had not engaged the enemy yet. This impatience did lead to an overall delay in the project, which is exactly what he was trying to avoid.

Curtius, several times, tells us of another key factor with regard to the mole: it was unstable.[106] Great efforts had been made, as noted above, to ensure the mole was structurally sound, but the sand was likely very soft and the boulders probably continued to sink slowly after Alexander's engineers had believed that they were solidly fixed in position. The likely instability of the foundations would not have been initially apparent until the massive extra weight of the siege towers was placed upon it. If I am correct in suggesting that the larger boulders continued to sink into the sand, albeit at a slow rate, then the mole would probably have been more stable closer to the shore where they had had the greatest time to settle into position, and most unstable at the construction face. If this is correct, then once the massive extra weight of the siege towers was added, it is no surprise at all that the mole became more unstable. The instability of the mole would have been increased by the prevailing winds in both directions, and by the waves it created. The effect of weather upon the mole is highlighted by Curtius when he mentions a severe storm that caused a considerable amount of damage to the mole, none of which is found in Arrian.[107]

Naval assaults by marines aboard triremes were no longer effective in disrupting the mole once the screens had been built, and were in fact far more dangerous for the Tyrian sailors given the presence of the newly-built defensive towers and presumably increased patrols on the mole. The Tyrians at this point could see the mole growing ever longer and progressing closer and closer to the walls of the fortress and they determined that they needed to take more direct action. The mole itself would be difficult to destroy, but progress could be interrupted. The siege towers, being made of wood, were an obvious and inviting target; their destruction would allow naval raids on the construction workers to continue uninterrupted, and progress would be seriously slowed once again. In order to achieve this they again showed their innovative spirit by filling:[108]

a cattle-boat with dry brushwood and various sorts of timber which would burn well, set up twin masts in her bows, and, as far as they could, raised her bulwarks all round in order to make her hold as much inflammable material as possible, including pitch, sulphur, and anything else which would burn fiercely.

Athenian horse transport vessels of the fourth century were essentially hollowed out triremes, basically the same design as the standard war ship but with the lower banks of oars removed to create space for the horses. The Tyrian vessel described by Arrian does not appear to have been of this expected design.[109] This vessel may have started out life as a standard warship, a trireme or more likely something larger, but it was further modified to fulfil a very specific purpose. The sides of the vessel were raised in order that it could carry more inflammable material, and presumably every bank of oars had been removed to provide even more space.

Although Arrian mentions brushwood in the so-called fireship, it is hard to see where such material could have come from in the island city. It is unlikely to have been specifically imported, and therefore timber from buildings was far more likely to be the primary incendiary material.

Arrian goes on to describe the accelerant used in the fire:[110]

Across the twin masts they rigged a yard double the usual length, and slung from it cauldrons full of any material which could be poured or flung on the fire to increase its fury, and, finally, heavily ballasted the vessel aft in order to lift her bows as high as possible. Then having waited for a fair wind, they passed hawsers to a number of triremes and towed her stern-first to the mole. Before she struck, the men in her leapt overboard and swam to safety.

The mast was, like the vessel herself, larger than the usual design; this was again almost certainly a bespoke mast designed specifically to allow the suspension of as many cauldrons of flammable material as possible. The fireship is a fine example of ancient chemical warfare.

It had evidently occurred to the Tyrians that it was likely, or at least possible, that the ship would simply run aground on the edges of the mole without getting close enough to the towers to do any real damage. The device of significantly overloading the aft of the vessel with rocks and sand in order to raise the bows out of the water and allow the vessel to essentially land the front section of the ship on land and extend the range of the fire to the siege towers was an ingenious solution to a potentially very difficult problem. Again the Tyrian defenders show themselves to be innovative and inventive in their defence.[111]

Delivering the fireship to its target was still problematic, however. Towing it from the front was difficult, partly because the fore of the vessel was out of the water and partly because the tow ropes would have to be detached before the tug-triremes ran aground themselves. There was also no guarantee that such a heavily laden vessel would maintain enough momentum to beach sufficiently to cause the desired destruction of the siege towers. Arrian does seem to imply that the fireship was towed from the stern, that is to say, from the rear of the vessel. This act is difficult to imagine but it does not seem to mean a pushing motion, but rather that the ropes were tied to the rear of the ship and the triremes would have been essentially alongside the fireship as they were pulling it. In this, they were assisted greatly by a following wind, evidently something they had been waiting for as it would further provide momentum to allow the fireship to run aground as far as possible. Whilst being towed, the marines on the fireship could ensure that the vessel was steered in the correct direction, and momentum could be maintained almost up to the point where the fireship was beached. The direction of the tug-triremes could relatively easily be reversed in order to get to a safe distance once the vessel was fired. These tug-triremes could then also pick up the marines that would have been in the water and who escaped once the vessel was fired.

The prevailing wind would not only have made it easier to tow the fireship onto the mole, but, once ablaze, the flame would have spread over a greater distance south of the ship (the attack came from the Sidonian harbour to the north), and therefore increase the likelihood of success by ensuring that the flame reached the siege towers. The flame on the fireship would have burned with incredible ferocity, but likely would have taken a few minutes to built up to its maximum intensity, more than enough time for the marines on board to make their escape, and the trireme tug-boats to row to safety. Arrian tells us:[112]

> Near the two towers they started the fire, and the crews of the triremes pulled with all their might until they flung the blazing cattle-boat on the edge of the mole. Before she struck the men in her leapt overboard and swam to safety.

The attack was timed to perfection and, with the help of the following wind, the two siege towers were quickly ablaze, the flame retardant coverings nowhere near sufficient to resist the intensity of the flame. The Tyrians' strategy was threefold, however; the second element was an order for the triremes that had acted as tug-boats to stay relatively close to the towers, presumably one vessel to the north and the other to the south of the mole. The marines onboard these vessels had orders to fire arrows at the defenders who would have been rushing towards the fireship with the intention of dousing the flame. This suppressing fire helped keep the defenders away from the fireship and the towers as the flame was taking its hold. But one has to imagine that their efforts would have been ineffective anyway against the soon-to-be-raging inferno. The real intention of the defenders was probably not to attempt to put out the fire onboard the ship (which would have quickly become far too intense for this to be feasible), but to drag the presumably-wheeled towers back along the mole to safety. I say the towers were presumably wheeled else they would have to be dismantled and rebuilt every hundred metres, or probably less, in order to maintain the protection of the forward working parties. In any event, their efforts failed and the towers were quickly ablaze.

Once the towers were fully ablaze, the Tyrians unleashed the third and final element of their strategy; as many of the defenders as they could manage, boarded triremes and sallied forth towards the mole, landing at pre-arranged points all along its length. Their intention was to cause as much chaos and destruction as was possible. Their primary target was the defensive palisades built along either side of the mole; with these destroyed they could resume their naval attacks with impunity. Other marine units were assigned to destroy the various artillery pieces that the Macedonians had stationed along the mole to help protect the construction crews. These attacks were devastatingly successful and once complete, the Tyrians quickly boarded their vessels and sailed back to the safety of the city having achieved exactly what they set out to achieve.[113] The Tyrian sortie was well planned and brilliantly executed; each of the three separate stages of the assault was well timed and executed with precision and discipline. Alexander and the Macedonians were seemingly taken completely by surprise; they evidently reacted slowly and were not able to prevent even the landings on the mole. This is a surprise, as the triremes carrying the marines would have been spotted by the troops on the mainland as they left the two harbours and would have taken some minutes to reach the mole. This lack of response suggests that the attack was timed to coincide with the lunch break of the Macedonians. We know from later in the siege that the attackers retired to the shore at midday every day to eat and rest. The Tyrians had evidently noticed this tendency and exploited it to their advantage, leaving a trail of death and destruction in their wake.

At the same time as the attack on the mole, Alexander's foraging parties came under attack from Arab tribesmen on Mt. Libanus. Curtius tells us that thirty Macedonians were killed and several taken prisoner.[114] There seems no particular reason to assume a coordinated resistance against the Macedonians; there was no reason that Arab peasants living in the mountains of Lebanon would wish to risk their lives for the citizens of wealthy Tyre. This was probably just an unfortunate coincidence; Alexander's foragers were perhaps taking too much from the land and leaving nothing for the Arabs, or else they were foraging where they were not supposed to be. Either way, the effect was morale destroying when coupled with the actions of the Tyrians against the mole.

However well planned a military engagement is, it can always go wrong. The

Tyrians' luck had held during the sortie, however, and that situation continued in the immediate aftermath of the attack. A massive and violent storm struck the mole and lasted for several hours during which time the mole was almost completely destroyed. Any remaining siege engines and defensive palisades were swept away and huge sections of the mole simply disappeared into the sea. The wooden pylons that had been driven into the sea bed to hold the large boulders in place were torn out, and the stone that had taken several months of hard toil (the Greeks apparently had not yet invented the wheelbarrow) to get into position fell away, destroying the mole almost completely.

The attack involving the fire ship was a crucial event during the siege of Tyre: the cause of the Macedonians was set back probably months; the Tyrians had struck a devastating blow with little loss of life to themselves. The sources present a picture of Alexander acting immediately to reconstruct the mole, but it is more likely that he took a little time to consider his options. When the metaphorical dust settled, Alexander was left with the same choice he had had at the start of the siege: capture the city by some means, or leave a now distinctly hostile naval base in enemy hands, and the stain of defeat upon his reputation. After a short period of introspection, Alexander gave orders to his engineers that the mole be rebuilt, but this time with new specifications.[115] The new mole was to be considerably wider than the one destroyed, although what remained of the first would have acted as the foundation for the central section. This extra space that would be created on the mole was intended to do several things. On the one hand, provide more stability in the event of another storm, but also to allow for the construction and deployment of more siege towers and artillery pieces to protect it and its workers. Two massive siege towers were also to be built on the mole; these were amongst the largest in the entire annals of ancient history. The new stability of the mole, and the fact that it could evidently cope with the added weight of these towers is another testimony to the ability of Alexander's famous engineers. Along with the offensive machinery on the mole, the defensive palisades that stretched down each side of the mole were to be rebuilt. These were evidently very effective in preventing naval archers and slingers from attacking the construction workers.

After leaving specific instructions for the reconstruction project under the command of Perdiccas, Alexander left Tyre for an expedition to Sidon, just to the north.[116] With him were a relatively small number of troops, only the Agrianians and hypaspists, perhaps 4,000 men in total. Alexander evidently did not expect trouble from the areas that were already under his control.

It seems that it was only now that Alexander was finally forced to accept that without a fleet he had little hope of capturing the island fortress.[117] He would have reasoned that if he did possess a fleet, he would be able to attack the island from multiple directions simultaneously; this was how he ultimately managed to capture the city, but he needed a fleet in order to make it possible. The failure to follow this strategy at the outset of operations seems like a mistake by Alexander, but his lack of a fleet made it impossible initially.

At the time of the orders to reconstruct the mole and the expedition to Sidon, Curtius presents us with a picture of a very depressed and disillusioned Alexander, a man undecided whether to continue with the siege, or to abandon it completely, his decision to stay only coming with the arrival of the Cypriot fleet.[118] This is almost certainly another instance of Curtius misunderstanding or misrepresenting his sources. It is likely that Alexander considered leaving, but not that he considered abandoning the siege altogether. He could never admit that he had been beaten, and thus Tyre had to fall. I see little reason to doubt, however, that Alexander himself considered leaving Tyre in order to campaign elsewhere, perhaps with Perdiccas or some other senior commander left in charge. Alexander could have done this in order to either chase Darius into the Persian heartlands as he had failed to do after Issus, or more likely to continue his naval policy by advancing into Egypt to capture the remainder of the Persian naval bases. Alexander was a man of action and sitting for several months while the mole was under construction, without being able to engage the enemy at all, would have been unbelievably frustrating for him. We do have an example of a similar action, the siege of Halicarnassus. Here Alexander did leave before the final fall of the city to continue the campaign, leaving Ptolemy and a detachment of troops behind to complete the capture. There may well have been discussions along these lines which Curtius has confused and conflated.

When Alexander had marched through the Persian naval bases to the north of Tyre, in every instance the king or ruler of the city was away with his fleet fulfilling his obligation as part of the Persian navy. When each of these individual kings heard about the fall of their home city, they abandoned the Persian fleet to return home. This essentially meant that the Persian fleet had almost entirely disbanded (some islands like Rhodes were still loyal to Darius, however). Once Alexander arrived at Sidon and made the request (or order) for the fleets to reform and join him, many of the commanders and navies of these recently conquered cities joined Alexander at Sidon. Gierostratus, king of Aradus, and Enylus, king of Byblos, both arrived after leaving the fleet of Autophradates. On a single day eighty Phoenician triremes arrived at Sidon, along with nine from Rhodes, three from Soli and Mallus, ten from Lycia and a fifty-oared vessel from

Macedonia. Shortly after this the kings of Cyprus arrived with 120 warships. Alexander accepted all of these vessels and their commanders with open arms, regardless of previous allegiance, as he recognized his immediate need if he was to complete the reduction of Tyre. Alexander's fleet, according to Arrian's numbers, almost overnight numbered 224 warships, a figure roughly in agreement with Plutarch's figure of 200 and Curtius' statement that Alexander used 190 in the final assault against Tyre.[19]

Alexander was now in possession of the most powerful fleet in the Aegean; this is exactly what his strategy of conquering the Persian navy on land was intended to achieve, and it had worked brilliantly. It must be said, however, that if Memnon had lived longer and carried through his plan of taking the war to Greece by using the Persian fleet to land troops there, the history of Alexander's career could have been completely different. From the moment of Alexander's acquisition of the former Persian fleet, the fate of Tyre was sealed.

The newly formed fleet would have taken time to both arrive and to organize once their allegiances had been assured. Whilst this was happening, presumably under the watchful eye of several senior Macedonian officers, Alexander took the opportunity for some light relief from the siege. He took a detachment of cavalry, the hypaspists, Agrianians and archers on an expedition into the Lebanese mountains. The cavalry were presumably light cavalry, as the Companions are not mentioned as being present on the expedition north to Sidon, and they surely would have been worthy of note.[120] These were invariably the troops that Alexander used for these sorts of rapid expeditions, where lightning fast movement and flexibility of arms were required. For ten days he conducted operations in mountainous terrain. The reasons are twofold. Alexander wanted to establish a supply of timber and other raw materials for the siege works (massive amounts of wood were no doubt being consumed by the mole and the siege engines, particularly given the recently-increased size of the project, as well as the wood that was required for cooking fires and heating). Alexander also wanted to relieve his own frustrations and those of his men after being unable to engage the Tyrians properly.[121] There is also a revenge motif of course, as these were the same Arabs that had killed thirty of his men while out foraging a month or two previously. This expedition against the Arabs almost certainly took place during the visit to Sidon, and not just prior to the attack of the fire ship as in Curtius.[122] Placing the expedition just before the destruction of the mole is an obvious device on the part of Curtius to remove any blame from Alexander for the disaster by having him away on expedition in the Lebanese mountains at the time.[123] Once Alexander returned to Sidon, his thirst for conquest sated for the time being, he found Cleander waiting with 4,000 much-needed Greek mercenary reinforcements from the Peloponnese.

The second and decisive phase of the siege began as Alexander embarked his men onboard ship. In order to make the grandest re-entrance possible to Tyre, he embarked as many foot soldiers as could be crammed into his new ships and set off south. The remainder of the troops were sent back to Tyre on foot. The delay in their arrival would not matter as the bulk of the army was already at Tyre. Within the new fleet, Alexander was in command of the right wing and Pyntagoras, king of Cyprus in command of the left. Pyntagoras was given such a prestigious position because his was the largest contingent of the new fleet. Command of such a large force showed a considerable degree of faith and trust in Alexander's new allies and was something of a risk, although if a national naval contingent was to revolt, it would make little difference where they were stationed or who was in command. Alexander's position on the right wing is indicative of his upbringing; it was always the case in land warfare that the place of honour in a land battle was on the right, such as the Spartans at Plataea, and we know that Alexander always fought on the right with the Companion Cavalry during his great set-piece battles. This organization probably again indicates Alexander's lack of naval experience. As noted at Halicarnassus, if Alexander was to have fought a naval battle (there or here), he likely would have tried to turn it into effectively a land battle fought at sea. This is not really surprising as there is nothing in Alexander's career or upbringing that would have prepared him for naval actions. Philip was no admiral either, and his Athenian allies did not provide any experienced crews at all. Alexander also would have been unsure of the advice he was receiving from his new allies. He also likely would have been keen to assert his dominant position over these new allies by giving them instructions, rather than acting on their advice, if indeed they offered any.

As the newly-constituted fleet sailed south, the Tyrians became aware of their approach, presumably by means of scouting vessels patrolling the region, a precaution no doubt started when it became apparent that the former Persian fleet had disbanded. As soon as they realized that enemy vessels approached, they sailed out to meet them on open water. The Tyrians evidently expected this to be only the Sidonian fleet after having seen Alexander head north in that direction perhaps a week or two previously. This is an indication of the strength of the Tyrian fleet, that they felt they could successfully engage the Sidonians. As soon as they realized that Alexander's new fleet was around 200 strong, and considerably outnumbered their own, they immediately turned around and made all speed for the safety of Tyre. What followed was a desperate race to see who could reach the harbours first. The Tyrian vessels were heavily laden and running low in the water because of the numbers of marines that were on board each vessel. This excess weight meant that they were cumbersome and slow to turn, as well as being far slower in a straight line than the lighter ships of Alexander's fleet. If Alexander's ships arrived at Tyre first, they could disembark their troops and capture the city while the bulk of the city's fighting men were on board ship.

Three of the Tyrian vessels were overtaken by Alexander's triremes; it is not clear if they deliberately turned to engage the Macedonians as a delaying tactic to allow the remainder to gain the ports safely, or if they were still running and were engaged by faster moving vessels; either way, all three Tyrian vessels were sunk after a brief naval skirmish. This did, however, buy enough time for the remainder of the Tyrian fleet to achieve the safety of the two ports. Once the Tyrians had reached the safety of the fortress, both ports were blockaded to prevent the possibility of Alexander gaining access.[124] This defensive tactic of the Tyrians is interesting; they were outnumbered, of this there is little doubt, but they undoubtedly would have operated with naval tactics superior to those of Alexander, given that he would have been reluctant to accept advice from his new allies/recent enemies (especially when we consider that he was so reluctant to even accept advice from the likes of Parmenio). It is likely that they simply felt the risk of an engagement was too great; if a naval battle was fought and lost, the defenders would not only have lost their fleet, but the majority of their fighting troops too, given that they were stationed with the fleet at the time.

It should be realized that the nature of the Tyrian tactics during the siege to this point can be described as cautiously ambitious. They had operated low-risk high-reward strategies; they were not gambling with the lives of everyone in the city. If the naval attacks against the mole had failed, few if any Tyrians would have died. Similarly with the incident of the fire ship; it was possible that some marines would be killed while trying to burn the siege engines and palisades, but the fleet was on hand to rescue anyone who dived into the sea to escape the inevitable Macedonian counter-offensive. The conservative stance in relation to a naval battle is not surprising, therefore. The Tyrians would also have realized that refusing to offer a fight on even terms would frustrate Alexander, perhaps to the point of acting rashly, something that they could exploit to their own advantage.

Once the Tyrian vessels were safely in the harbour, they turned their prows out towards the sea and lined themselves up along the mouth of their harbours so that no Macedonian vessel could gain access. Each ship was also still fully laden with defenders; Alexander saw this arrangement and decided not to attempt to force an entry; the risk of defeat, and the potential losses in ships and men was too high. Instead, Alexander moved the fleet to station on either side of the mole, and the following day a naval blockade of the island began. The Cypriot fleet took up a station opposite the northern Sidonian harbour, whilst the Phoenician contingent blockaded the Egyptian harbour to the south. The remainder of the fleet, specifically the Rhodian vessels, and what existed of the Macedonian fleet, were held in reserve and stationed alongside the mole to act as protection for the construction crews and as a reserve force in the event of a successful break out by the ships of Tyre. The ability to prevent food, water and reinforcements from reaching the city immediately gave Alexander the upper hand. The blockade also made it a far more risky proposition for the defenders to launch a sortie against the mole or the new siege towers and catapults as it drew ever closer to the city walls.

Construction now continued with renewed vigour; the construction teams no longer had to worry about attack, and the presence of a fleet presumably made logistics considerably easier. The mole was quickly widened as per Alexander's instructions; this evidently took far less time than the construction of the original mole because of their experience in building the first mole, and because it could be used as a foundation once it had been repaired. Not only was the mole widened, but the pace of progress towards Tyre also increased. During this phase of construction, another storm hit the mole, probably less severe than the first, but it certainly had the potential to set the project back again. Alexander had seen the destruction caused by the first storm and this time set in place measures to mitigate the damage. He had a number of whole trees cut down and floated in the sea to either side of the mole. The intention being that the branches would break up the force of the waves to such an extent that the damage would be limited. The felled trees must have been secured in some way; else the force of the waves would simply have sent them crashing against the mole, probably causing more damage than the waves would have alone. Either way, the device was successful and only minor damage was sustained. This was quickly repaired and progress was soon underway again.[125] The lack of damage is also suggestive of the improved quality and stability of the extended mole over the earlier one. Lessons must have been learned during the early construction that was being applied to the latter.

It is of this second phase of construction that our sources provide us with almost no information. Arrian presents a picture of the arrival of the new fleet and in the next paragraph the mole was virtually at the walls of Tyre, within missile range at least.[126] There must have been a gap of at least a couple of months to allow for the repairs and extensions to the mole that had been ordered after the destruction of the first set of siege towers by the fire ship. This time was used wisely by Alexander; the mole occupied the attentions of a major part of his workforce, especially the newly-drafted men from Cyprus and Phoenicia. Many of his engineers were engaged in building the massive siege towers and building large numbers of catapults and other siege engines. These engineers were not only working on mundane engines, but were also constructing catapults that were mounted on triremes to be used at sea. These catapults were evidently of both arrow-throwing and stone-throwing varieties. Alexander apparently also had triremes lashed together and siege towers built on their decks; Curtius tells us that they were lashed at their prows to form a delta shape with planks connecting the two, upon which stood the siege tower.[127] This remarkably precarious situation could not have supported a particularly tall tower, but missiles launched from a greater height were more likely to have had an impact upon the defenders than arrows launched from sea level. These ship-borne artillery pieces and towers were intended to act in coordination with marines on troop transport vessels. These would have been equipped with scaling ladders that were raised from a turret, not unlike the larger naval siege towers, the intention being that the artillery would lay down a suppressing fire against the defenders and allow the marines to climb the walls unhindered.

Once the mole was within range, Alexander ordered the siege proper to begin both from the mole and from ships at every point around the circumference of the fortress. The Tyrians had not sat upon their laurels while the mole was being constructed, however; they had themselves built defensive equivalents of Alexander's siege towers on the battlements. The intention of these towers was to be higher than Alexander's siege towers so that they could reign down arrows and artillery fire upon the attackers, and essentially to attempt to prevent them from doing the same. The Tyrians also stationed their own artillery and missile troops at every point around the circuit of the city where they were under attack and answered with missile fire of their own.[128] Fire arrows were used against anything potentially flammable, particularly against Alexander's navy when a vessel strayed too close (a necessity if they were to use their own projectile weapons). These fire arrows were so successful that the crews of some ships were afraid to approach too close to the fortress.

The defenders again showed their inventiveness in a couple of other creations; firstly they set up what would have looked like windmills along some stretches of the walls; these continuously rotating devices would act as anti-catapult weapons. Arrows, both from bowmen and catapults would hit the sails of the windmills as they rotated and would be deflected before reaching the defenders. This was an extremely clever device and was in some ways more effective than a simple screen as it would allow the defenders to fire when the gaps between the blades was in front of them. The defenders also used large shields placed over fires and filled with sand. This boiling hot sand was then dropped upon the attackers as they attempted to scale ladders. If the attackers had been wearing any armour at all, even a leather tunic, it would have been impossible to prevent red hot sand from being trapped against the skin; one can only imagine how agonizing this must have been, especially when halfway up a ladder and with no means of quenching the tortuous heat.[129]

The walls closest to the mainland were by far the tallest and strongest; when the fortress was constructed the builders could not have conceived of an attacker building a mole in order to besiege the island. What they no doubt intended was for the fortress to look impregnable, and therefore presented the strongest side to those viewing it from the mainland. This, of course, did have the corollary effect of making it almost impossible to carry the siege from the mole. To this end the naval vessels were becoming increasingly important as the mechanism through which victory would be achieved.

The defenders realized this too, and as an added layer of defence they had dropped large boulders into the sea all around the island. One can only imagine that sections of the city had been dismantled and destroyed in order to provide the stone that was used (and for the wood of the defensive siege towers). The situation with regards supplies and stockpiles of everything must have been desperate by this stage of operations. Alexander's troops made use of some of the boulders closest to the mole, slinging ropes around them and dragging them from the sea. They were then presumably incorporated into the ever-growing mole, despite Arrian's claim that they were then lifted by cranes and dropped into deeper water. What would be the point, if stones of these dimensions were being dragged from the mainland for the construction?[130] The stones in deeper water that could not be reached from the mole were more problematic.

Alexander's naval commanders who were attempting to clear away the boulders in deeper water in order to make a close approach of the walls became entangled in a game of cat and mouse with the defenders. In order to raise the rocks out of the ocean, the triremes had to be stationary to provide a stable working platform. In order to achieve any kind of stability, the ships had to be anchored; these anchor ropes were initially made of rope. Arrian goes on to tell us:[131]

> The Tyrians in certain specially-armoured vessels kept driving athwart the bows of the Macedonian triremes and cutting the anchor cables, so that it was impossible for them to remain in their station.

These Tyrian vessels are of unknown type, but they must have been smaller and more manoeuvrable than triremes. They probably had some form of bladed weapon protruding from the sides of the vessel, or perhaps crewmen simply slashed through the ropes as they passed close by the moored ships. Either way, as long as the Macedonians were not securely moored in place, they could not raise the rocks from the ocean, and therefore could not approach the walls as they had been ordered. Alexander's response to this is telling of his tactical thinking at this time: he fitted out a number of vessels and used them as a defensive screen against the Tyrian ships. This is exactly the tactic that he used to protect the workers on the mole, essentially the creation of a solid barrier. The Tyrians' response was to send a number of divers to cut the cables; these men would then swim back to the relative safety of the fortress. Alexander then substituted chain for the rope, against which the divers were ineffective.[132]

In this incident, as with earlier ones on the mole, we see Alexander reacting to actions of the defenders. This is certainly not the proactive innovator that we would expect. What we may have here is something we see elsewhere: when Alexander is confronted with an entirely-new situation for the first time, the outcome is usually less successful than in subsequent encounters in similar circumstances. We can see, for example, the struggles initially in the Balkans, at Halicarnassus and the island of Tyre juxtaposed with the later stunning successes at Gaza and during the eastern sieges. Alexander shows himself to be a commander who does not always instantly make the correct decisions when faced with a situation he has never seen, but quickly learns and adapts.

With the ships now properly protected, they continued to clear the area all around the circuit of the fortress of the stone that had been dropping there. As this work progressed, the Tyrians were becoming ever more desperate and had to adopt a higher risk strategy thant they had been comfortable with early in the siege: they resolved to attack the Cypriot fleet stationed to the north of the mole, outside of the Sidonian harbour.

The defenders had observed a curious recurring pattern in the behaviour of the attackers: at noon every day the crews of the Cyrpiot fleet to the north of the mole landed on the mainland to prepare and eat their lunchtime meal, as well as to take some rest. When this happened, only a small number of vessels were left blockading the northern harbour. At the same time Alexander, who was invariably stationed with the Egyptian fleet to the south, would also go ashore to take a midday break. The pattern seemed to repeat itself day after day, and the Tyrians saw an opportunity to deliver a hammer blow to the attackers and to resume naval attacks upon the mole. This was a high-risk strategy as the defenders had no means of replacing any ships or men that were lost if the attack did not go according to plan.

This kind of counter-attack during the enemy's lunch break was as old as Greek warfare; the defenders were hoping for the kind of impact that Lysander had had over the Athenian fleet at Aegospotami in 405.[133] On that occasion, the Athenians beached their vessels in order to search for food; Lysander did not do the same but kept his fleet ready. At the appropriate point, Lysander attacked the few triremes that were left at sea and quickly defeated them, following this up by the capture of almost the entire Athenian fleet of around 160 ships and their crews. It would not have been possible for the Tyrians to entirely replicate this success as the presence of a large army on land would prevent the capture of the ships and crews; the Egyptian fleet would also likely cause difficulties. The best the Tyrians could hope for was to destroy a significant part of the Macedonian fleet, which would cause a very considerably negative impact upon morale, as well as possibly breaking the siege to allow supplies into the beleaguered city.

It has been noted that, for a stratagem that was so common, it is very surprising that Alexander did not anticipate it and take steps to prevent it from occurring.[134] On the surface, this appears to be true, but we must look a little more closely. The Cypriot fleet did indeed retire to the shore every day at a specific time for lunch, and left only a few vessels at sea. It is also the case that the Egyptian fleet appears not to have done this. All Arrian tells us is that *Alexander* went ashore for a nap at lunch, not that the Egyptians joined him. What we have, therefore, is the situation that Alexander presents many times to his enemies, just on a different scale and in a different context. Alexander left a 'pawn-sacrifice' to lure the enemy onto ground of his choosing so he could quickly turn an attack from the enemy into a rapid and devastating counter-attack by his own men. The fact that the Egyptians were stationed to the south side of the mole and could easily sail around the island and cut off the Tyrians from their harbour if they were not very quick in their actions would be fundamental to this strategy. The final piece of evidence is that Alexander had, apparently, taken to not going ashore for his nap (perhaps once the screen had been rigged across the Sidonian harbour by the Tyrians a few weeks earlier), no doubt anticipating that his carefully-laid trap was about to be sprung.[135]

In order to hide their preparations from prying eyes, the defenders had erected a series of sails across the harbour mouth to prevent the Cypriots from seeing inside, as noted above; behind this screen preparations were finalized for his daring sortie. The screen must have been put into position at least a few days, and perhaps a week or two, before the naval sortie or the besiegers may have guessed something was about to occur. The Tyrian sortie fleet was quite small, probably an indication that they were running short of ships; these were four triremes, three quinquiremes and three quadriremes. These vessels were manned with:[136]

> Hand-picked crews – their smartest men, their best-armed marines, specially selected for their courage in naval warfare.

Once the final preparations had been made with as little noise as possible so as not to risk alerting the Cypriot vessels stationed outside the harbour, they organized themselves into single file, removed the sail screen from the harbour mouth, and slipped quietly out of the harbour entrance. The men at the oars made not a sound, and time was not called; they were as close to silent as could be achieved in an ancient navy. When they left the harbour mouth and turned to come within sight of the Cypriots, they raised an almighty roar of shouts and cheers and they made to attack the enemy with all speed.

What the Tyrians encountered were Cypriot ships that were either empty or had mere skeleton crews on board. Three Cypriot quinquiremes were sunk immediately and many others were driven onto the beach and disabled.[137] One of the ships that was rammed and sunk quickly was the flagship of King Pyntagoras of Cyprus, although he was not on board at the time. The remainder of the vessels that were not immediately sunk were driven onto the shore. After the success against the remaining ships, the Tyrians evidently made to attack some of the beached vessels, with their marines disembarking and starting a number of fires. It is interesting to note that the fleet was the primary target of the sortie, not the catapults and towers on the mole this time. This is a clear indication that the primary purpose was to break the naval blockade and allow supply vessels to enter the city once more. They were more worried about this than about the mole. It is also a probable indication that the defenders feared naval attacks more than those from the mole, suggesting that Alexander's naval siege weapons were highly effective and perhaps that the walls away from the mole were far weaker than those opposing it.

As it happens, either by chance or by a designed trap, Alexander had not taken his usual afternoon nap, but had returned to the Phoenician fleet almost immediately after his trip to shore. One can only assume that the trip was made

exander's capture of Miletus (by André Castaigne, first published 1898).

The Myndus Gate, now restored, is the only surviving section of the walls of Halicarnassus besieged by Alexander the Great. (*courtesy of www.Livius.org*)

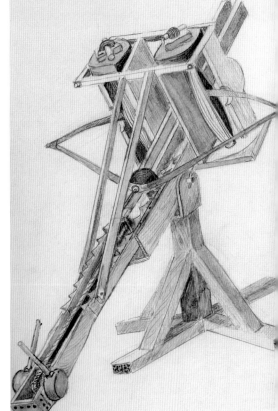

The torsion catapults used by Alexander's army were at the cutting edge of siege technology. (*after Jeff Burn, © J. Sidnell*)

wo views of the surviving 4th-century BC walls of Assos in Turkey, showing how formidable rtifications of this time could be. These still stand to a height of 13m in places.

Alexander's mole is attacked by ships during his siege of Tyre (drawn by Didier and engraved by W. Roberts, circa 1848). (© *Andrew Michael Chugg, www.alexanderstomb.com*)

A Macedonian assault directed by Alexander during the siege of Tyre (plate 7 of 11 on the deeds of Alexander by Antonio Tempesta of Florence, published in 1608).

(© *Andrew Michael Chugg, www.alexanderstomb.com*)

Engraved view of Tyre looking seawards, along the mole, before modern development (engraved by Petit and first published in 1889).
(© *Andrew Michael Chugg, www.alexanderstomb.com*)

A naval action during the siege of Tyre. In the background, huge siege towers can be seen on the mole (by André Castaigne, 1898–1899).
(© *Andrew Michael Chugg, www.alexanderstomb.com*)

In the classical period, Lade (NW of Miletus) was a strategically-vital island; now the island is connected to the mainland because of the River Meander silting up over the centuries. The three peaks of the former island can still be seen. (*courtesy of www.Livius.org*)

The Persian Gates. Alexander marched thousands of men, at night, through the mountains to turn the Persian fortification.

(*courtesy of www.Livius.org*)

Aornus (Pir-Sar) from the southeast, with the River Indus in the foreground.
(*courtesy of www.Livius.org*)

Aornus (Pir-Sar) from the northwest, with the River Indus in the foreground.
(*courtesy of www.Livius.org*)

The ladder breaks stranding Alexander and a few companions on the walls of th Mallian town (by André Castaigne, first published 1899). (© *Andrew Michael Chugg, www.alexanderstomb.com*)

Alexander's lone defence against the Mallians/Oxydracae after leaping down within its walls (anonymous illustration from De Vaugelas' French translation of Curtius, published in Amsterdam in 1696). (© *Andrew Michael Chugg, www.alexanderstomb.com*)

to trick the Tyrians into thinking this was an entirely normal day, exactly the same as the many previous days when this behaviour had been observed. Upon hearing of the sortie, presumably be means of a pre-arranged signal from men stationed on the mole, he ordered the Egyptian harbour to be sealed lest another attack be launched from there, and sailed with the remainder of the Phoenician fleet to the relief of the Cyprians. The defenders manning the walls of the city frantically shouted and tried to signal those in the ships, but to no avail, their attention was fixed upon the Cyprian fleet. Most of the attacking Tyrian vessels were either captured or sunk as they failed to make the safety of the harbour before being engaged by Alexander, although the loss of life was small as the sailors simply swam to safety. The further loss of warships was another crippling blow for the defenders. All hope that the Tyrians had of gaining some measure of protection from their fleet was now gone and the tide of the siege had well and truly turned against the defenders.[138]

Soon after the unsuccessful sortie, the construction workers on the mole managed to complete their works to the point that the mole now touched the very walls of the city:[139]

> The Tyrians had their present danger before their eyes and easily imagined what a disaster the actual capture of the city would be, so that they spent themselves so freely in the contest as to despise mortal danger.

At this point, a general artillery bombardment was ordered all round the circuit of the city. This, as noted earlier, was one of Alexander's hallmark techniques, and was ordered here partly as a means of reducing the numbers of defenders stationed at the walls, and partly as a means of probing for a weak spot in the city's defences. Once the Macedonians' barrage was finally underway, archers were stationed upon the giant siege towers with orders to rain a constant stream of arrows towards the battlements in an attempt to prevent the defenders from retaliating or reorganizing themselves. The artillery bombardment from the mole was to no avail, however, as the walls were far too thick in that sector to be seriously damaged by ancient catapults. Alexander then seems to have attempted to concentrate his naval artillery, now that the rocks had been cleared from the sea around the city, against the northern sector of the walls, whilst still maintaining some actions against the other sectors. Naval battering rams were also employed from a close range, but again to no avail as the walls were again too thick. These rams were mounted between two ships with some form of protective shed built over the top to afford them some measure of protection from overhead fire; the vessels and the rams were also covered in fire-retardant skins, as were the towers.

Along with the naval bombardment, troop transports lay just out of missile range lest a breakthrough could be achieved. After relative failure in the northern sector, the attentions of the naval assault turned south in what Arrian describes as 'feeling methodically for a weak spot', with rather more success this time.[140] A considerable length of wall shook after a prolonged assault and finally collapsed. Once the wall had partially collapsed, Arrian presents a picture of an abortive naval assault:

> Alexander then made a tentative attack – a probing movement, not much more, in point of fact, than the throwing of a bridge across the breach. The movement was easily repulsed.

Both Curtius and Diodorus give us a rather more vivid picture of the assault, particularly in the southern sector of the city. The Tyrians poured down flame, arrow, javelins and stones upon the attackers, wherever they met them; in fact anything they could lay their hands upon as their very lives, and the lives of their families, were in the balance. In order to try to free the rams from the walls (they had been tethered to the walls by means of ropes), the defenders lowered long poles with sharp blades attached to the end to cut the mooring ropes. They also had developed a form of flame thrower, perhaps of a similar design to that employed by the Spartan King Brasidas during the Peloponnesian War. Using this device, the Phoenicians spewed fire and molten metal upon the attackers, and given that they were tightly packed (especially on the mole and in the breach), they did immense damage; many died and more were badly mutilated. This flame thrower was truly a terror weapon, far more so than the catapult. The Macedonians apparently did not falter, but kept advancing, even when they saw their comrades ahead of them fall.[141]

> Alexander mounted the stone throwing catapults in the proper places (i.e. on the mole, and onboard ship) and made the walls rock with the boulders that they threw. With the dart-throwers on the wooden towers he kept up a constant fire of all kinds of missiles and terribly punished the defenders of the walls.

It was as a response to this constant attack that the defenders rigged up the windmills, which Diodorus notes as being of marble construction, to constantly rotate and knock these smaller arrows and darts out of the air. They also used the boiling sand at this point against the attackers, and filled hides with seaweed and suspended these from the walls in an attempt to cushion the blow of the stone throwers; these are fine examples of innovation borne of desperation. Diodorus goes on to say that the Tyrians were:[142]

> Bold in the face of their enemies, and left the shelter of the walls and their positions within the towers to push out onto the very bridges (from the ships) and match the courage of the Macedonians with their own valour. They grappled with the enemy and, fighting hand to hand, put up a stout battle for their city. Some of them used axes to chop off any part of the body of an opponent that presented itself.

The naval assault had lasted until nightfall, and Alexander called a withdrawal. Diodorus and Curtius are almost certainly correct in presenting the fighting at the breach as being fierce and vicious; it is inconceivable that after a nine-month siege with the elite hypaspists given the opportunity to engage the enemy on land, or at least a breach in a wall for the first time, that they would not embrace this opportunity with open arms. Arrian's description of troops being reticent to fight seems unlikely. Their only reluctance may have come from the thought of the flame throwers, boiling sand etc, and not at the thought of battle as such.

After the initial assault was repulsed at the breach in the southern wall, there was a lull in the fighting. Diodorus tells us that Alexander made an offer to accept the surrender of Tyre. The offer, if real, was not popular amongst the Macedonian high command; only Amyntas supported it. The Tyrians were given two days to surrender; on the third day the final assault began. A delay is also attested in Arrian, although he attributes it to bad weather, and in Curtius where the chronology of the final stages is confused and difficult to follow.[143]

Curtius also tells us that Alexander seriously considered abandoning the siege altogether after the repulse at the walls, and heading south towards Egypt. He goes on to say that:[144]

> After sweeping through Asia at a headlong pace he was now detained before the walls of a single city, with so many magnificent opportunities lost.

It is difficult to see what these opportunities were specifically, especially in the light of his future conquests. It is highly unlikely that Alexander considered such an option at this stage: this section of Curtius' narrative owes rather more to romance than history; Curtius also tells us of a huge sea creature that rose from the waters and came to rest upon the mole.[145]

We can reasonably believe that Curtius has made a mistake. Alexander almost certainly did not consider abandonment, but simply retired for the day as evening was drawing close in order to rest his troops and regroup for a renewed assault the following morning. Curtius is probably confused with an earlier point in the siege, perhaps the destruction of the mole by the device of the fireship.

The final assault began with an artillery barrage, which was essentially a precursor of those that were to become so common during World War II offensives. After the naval barrage, two sectors were targeted for close assault: the harbour entrances and the breach.[146]

> Some of his triremes he ordered round to the two harbours, on the chance that they might succeed in forcing an entrance while the enemy's attention was engaged in trying to repel the assault elsewhere; other vessels which had archers on board or carried ammunition for the artillery were instructed to cruise round the island and, wherever they could, close in with the wall, lying off but within range if it so happened that to get close in was impossible, so that the defenders might be threatened from every point and caught, as it were, in a ring of fire.

In terms of understanding Alexander's strategy, this paragraph of Arrian is crucial. It spells out plainly and clearly one of Alexander's hallmark strategies, namely attacking the enemy from multiple directions simultaneously. At Tyre, during the final assault, it worked brilliantly, as it did in all of Alexander's encounters.

The naval barrage was conducted all around the walls of the city; once complete, a *taxis* of hypaspists under Admetus attacked the breach. Admetus was killed by a spear before gaining the walls, but Alexander, who was also present, pressed forward and soon the southern sector of the city walls was in Macedonian hands. It is clear from our sources that the troops were well drilled and commanded: they did not simply pour into the city as may have been expected, but remained in the vicinity of the walls to ensure the breach was held as more troops were brought forward after landing from the troop transports held just out of missile range.[147]

The breach that was assaulted appears to be larger during this final assault than it had been during the earlier repulsed attack, although likely not down to the foundations as Diodorus suggests.[148] On this occasion we are told that Alexander took personal control of one of the groups of attackers, and that the section of wall that was attacked by Alexander was where the breakthrough occurred. As Alexander broke through with some members of the hypaspists, he quickly spread out and captured several towers along the southern stretch of the walls. The Macedonians seem to have taken some time to secure their gains on the walls before proceeding into the city. This was sensible given the relative lack of troops that Alexander would have had with him at the time due to the limited transport capacity of ancient triremes. Once he did decide to expand his bridgehead, he made his way around ever greater sections of the walls and made for the royal quarter of the city.

Whilst the assault on the breach had been occurring, the fleet had performed no less well. The Phoenician fleet that was stationed opposite the Egyptian harbour broke through the defensive boom that lay across the harbour and made short work of what remained of the Tyrian fleet inside; these vessels were rammed and sunk without significant loss of life among the Phoenicians. The Cypriot fleet to the north was equally successful, and their task was made easier by the lack of any defensive booms across the harbour mouth. Marines aboard both navies quickly landed and gained control of these sectors of the city.

Once the defenders all across the city saw that time was running out, that sections of the walls were in enemy hands, along with the harbours, they abandoned their positions and took sanctuary in the shrine of Agenor, the father of Cadmus, who was the legendary founder of both Tyre and Sidon. Their intention was of making a last stand; Alexander did not disappoint them. Arrian tells us the slaughter was terrible, the Macedonians were allowed to vent their fury at such a brutal siege upon the survivors. Some 8,000 Tyrians were killed and the remaining 30,000 were sold into slavery, as was the usual practice.[149]

The creation of the mole was a tremendous feet of engineering and was achieved without drafting in specialists from Greece; Alexander had the foresight to bring with him construction experts for just such an unusual situation. Of almost equal difficulty, but always overshadowed by the mole, were the construction of the two great siege towers at the end of the mole itself. These must have been static towers, and capable of stationing stone- and arrow-throwing catapults inside them. Alexander's engineering inventiveness is also demonstrated by the curious siege engines that were created from former triremes and transport vessels: artillery, siege towers, ladders on platforms, rams etc. All of these helped in achieving victory, but it is a sobering thought that the final successful attack upon the city came from a ship-borne assault, and not from the mole itself, or from the siege towers. One could conclude that these were a massive folly and not ultimately necessary, but this is to miss the point. They were instrumental in forcing the Tyrians to station large numbers of defenders opposite the mole and thus reduce the potential numbers of defenders at other more vulnerable areas.

The capture of Tyre is usually regarded as the finest achievement of Alexander's military career. This is not without some justification. Tyre was a seemingly-impregnable island fortress that was heavily defended and commanded by an extremely-talented king, Azemilcus. When we closely examine the events of the siege, however, we see that many of Alexander's great innovations were in fact enforced reactions to Tyrian inventiveness. We see Alexander making a series of key errors or misjudgements, such as pushing forward construction work on the mole at the expense of defending it properly, which led to its destruction and a major delay. We also see Alexander's lack of creativity as an admiral, using essentially land-based tactics for his fleet. This said, however, Alexander certainly showed himself very capable of adapting to new situations and new defensive measures with increasingly-elaborate ideas of his own. That Alexander captured Tyre is beyond doubt and we should recognize that fact; the victory was due as much to persistence and the quality of his troops as it was to innovation. We should also note, as a final point, that king Azemilcus was one of the most able commanders he ever faced, and should be given the honour that he deserves.

Chapter 5
Gaza: 332

Tyre was no doubt one of Alexander's greatest military achievements, albeit not a series of unremitting victorious innovations as some may wish to suggest. However, the overall fact that he managed to capture a well-defended and brilliantly-commanded island fortress half a mile off the coast is an achievement that spans the ages. In terms of tactics, however, Gaza was at least as interesting, although always understandably overshadowed by the capture of Tyre a few months earlier. Gaza has consistently been ignored by historians both modern and ancient, most seeing it as little more than an interlude between the great siege of Tyre and the events in Egypt, but it certainly deserves far more attention than the couple of lines that Diodorus dedicated to the siege:[150]

> In this year (331/0) King Alexander set in order the affairs of Gaza and sent off Amyntas with ten ships to Macedonia, with orders to enlist the young men who were fit for military service.

I aim here to redress the balance somewhat, and give Gaza the position it deserves in the annals of Alexander's military career.

Aftermath of Tyre

Arrian tells us that towards the end of the siege of Tyre, Alexander received envoys from Darius offering peace terms.[151] Darius apparently offered Alexander the princely sum of 10,000 talents in gold in exchange for the safe return of his mother, wife and children who had all been captured after Darius' defeat at the Battle of Issus the previous year. Darius made the further proposal that Alexander should be ceded all territory west of the Euphrates, and that the alliance would be sealed by the marriage of Alexander to Darius' daughter, thus joining the royal houses of Persia and Macedonia and ensuring peaceful relations in the future.

Alexander received the offer in secrecy and did not immediately divulge it to his senior officers, nor did he immediately reply to Darius, perhaps giving the latter false hope that Alexander was intending to accept. Probably several days later, Alexander, at a regular meeting of his senior commanders, read out the contents of the letter, and we can only imagine the furore that must have ensued. As with any cabinet today, some would have favoured war and the annihilation of the Persian Empire, some would have favoured peace and a return home; each side would have made its feelings felt with vigour. This early in the campaign the commanders would almost certainly have felt relatively uninhibited about making their feelings known to the king; that would change over the course of the subsequent few years as Alexander became increasingly paranoid and insular. We do not know how long Alexander would have allowed the discussion and debate to rage, but we know of one significant proponent of peace: Parmenio. Arrian tells us that Parmenio:[152]

> According to all reports, declared that were he Alexander he would be happy to end the war on such terms and be done with any further adventures.

In this reply we can almost hear the voice of the ghost of Philip. Whilst we can never know with certainty how Philip would have reacted to this offer, he was always a man who used physical force only when necessary and seldom as a first response. Philip's stream of peace treaties with former enemies, and the string of wives that resulted, clearly illustrates his willingness to accept diplomatic solutions. It seems likely that Philip would at least have given the offer far more consideration than Alexander evidently did. Perhaps Alexander read the letter to his generals to gauge their enthusiasm for further conquest, or perhaps the story is apocryphal (it almost certainly occurred during Alexander's second visit to Tyre after the conquest of Egypt rather that at the end of the siege). Either way, his reported response to Parmenio is interesting:

> That is what I would do if I were Parmenio; but since I am Alexander, I shall send Darius a different answer.

Alexander apparently sent Darius a letter of reply; Arrian does not report the specific contents, but has the gist as follows:

He had no need, he wrote, of Darius' money, nor was there any call upon him to accept a part of the continent in place of the whole. All Asia, including its treasury, was already his property, and if he wished to marry Darius' daughter he would do so, whether Darius liked it or not. If, moreover, Darius wanted kindliness and consideration at his hands, he must come to ask for it in person. Upon receiving this reply, Darius abandoned all thought of coming to terms and began once more to prepare for war.

In all likelihood, the peace offer was genuine, even if the timing is disputed. Although the specific words of the letter and Alexander's reply are probably apocryphal, Arrian likely preserves the gist of what was said in both cases. The words of Alexander's reply do appear to be in keeping with what we would like to think we know of as his general character, although such arguments are always dangerous. Based upon the actions of the remainder of his career there is nothing to suggest he would have even seriously considered accepting such an offer; he probably saw it as a sign of weakness from Darius.

Was Alexander right to reject the offer? From the perspective of Darius, the offer was strategically very clever; Alexander did already own (almost) all of the territory that he offered and Darius' treasury would not miss 10,000 talents. Alexander was correct to say that he also already possessed Darius' wife and daughter, so the offer of marriage was an empty offer as he could not stop such a union if Alexander desired it. Further to this essentially-empty offer, if Alexander were to have accepted, Darius would have bought himself time to raise a new army to drive the invader from Persian lands; the nobility of Persia would surely have demanded this as long as the empire was even partially intact.

From Alexander's perspective, to accept would have been suicide. He could not possibly have defended a border stretching from the Black Sea to Egypt; this is to say nothing of the fact that significant parts of the army would no doubt have been disbanded as the war of revenge for Persian atrocities during the Persian Wars would then have been over. Alexander had no real strategic choice but to reject the offer. But again I would argue that even if it were strategically sound, Alexander would have rejected it anyway on the grounds of his *pothos* for further conquest, rather than peaceful government of the new territories as Augustus would have advocated.

After the successful capture of Tyre, Alexander was faced with essentially the same two strategic options he had had after the Battle of Issus: march inland in search of Darius and a final and decisive battle or continue following the coast into Egypt and complete the capture of the Persian naval bases, thus eliminating any possible danger from the Persian fleet. The earlier decision had been relatively straightforward; Alexander could not sensibly have left behind an active and powerful Persian fleet with the inherent danger of their carrying the war into mainland Greece – although this was, with the benefit of hindsight, unlikely after the untimely death of Memnon of Rhodes. For the safety and security of the growing empire, Tyre had to be in Macedonian hands. The fall of Tyre effectively meant that there was no longer a significant threat from the Persian navy; almost every ship in the combined Persian fleet had defected to the conqueror during the siege; what few remained were certainly no match for Alexander's newly acquired navy. The initial highly controversial strategy was no longer valid, yet Alexander decided to complete the reduction of Persian naval bases anyway by marching into Egypt. The question remains, however, why did Alexander not pursue Darius at this point and leave Egypt to its own devices?

There are a number of possible explanations; firstly it does not seem to be in Alexander's character profile to leave a potentially-powerful adversary unchallenged and unconquered. Egypt was a potential enemy, though an unlikely one given its historical resistance to Persian occupation. It is, of course, historically unsound to attempt to make too many judgements about the character of a man so long dead, we can never know what he truly thought and felt.

The second reason may be Alexander's desire to conquer the whole of the Persian Empire, of which Egypt was certainly part, albeit a reluctant and recalcitrant part. Cambyses first conquered Egypt in 525, and from around the middle of the fifth century (the time Herodotus was writing) successive Persian rulers were extremely unpopular there. In 404, Egypt successfully revolted from Persian rule, until a brutal re-conquest by Artaxerxes III Ochus in 341.

The lure of one of the great oracles of the ancient world would also have been very strong to Alexander. The oracle at Siwah was thought by Egyptians to be the home of Ammon, the head of the Egyptian pantheon, a figure that Greeks easily associated with Zeus.[153] We do not know what Alexander asked the oracle, or the reply, only that Alexander is thought to have said that he received the answer that he most wanted. This is likely to have been an answer to a question regarding his parentage, i.e. that Zeus was in fact his father, and that Alexander was, therefore, the son of a god. We may say, however, with the benefit of twenty-three centuries of distance, and with modern cynicism, that it is unlikely that a man like Alexander, who was in the process of conquering the Persian Empire, would have received any answer that he would have been unhappy hearing.

A final reason to move south against Egypt, and perhaps the most significant tactical and strategic reason of all, was the constant need for food, both for the army and to ensure Greece was well fed, eliminating a potential reason for revolt. Throughout the ancient world, Egypt was something of a bread basket for most of the Mediterranean region, from fifth-century Athens to the height of the Roman Empire. Alexander had a tremendous flair for logistics, as is evidenced by the lack of difficulties he had throughout his career. He seldom ran low on food or water, and this was partly because he took care of these essentials whenever he had the opportunity, as now.[154]

With the decision apparently an easy one, Alexander left some troops behind to act as a garrison in Tyre, as was the usual practice, and in this instance to help rebuild the city after the devastation of the siege, rested the army briefly and then set off south towards the next fortified position, Gaza.

Gaza was the principal frontier fortress of the Persian Empire in that region, around 240km south of Tyre, and 4km inland from the coast. For years it had stood guarding the Persian heartlands from aggression from an often-recalcitrant Egypt, and now it stood directly in Alexander's path *into* Egypt. From the perspective of the Macedonian conqueror, Gaza simply had to be captured; although Alexander probably had contact with what we would now call the Egyptian resistance, he could not be certain of the welcome he would receive. If the Egyptians ultimately proved to be hostile, Darius could easily trap him between Egypt and Palestine using Gaza as a forward base if he tried to march straight past it into Egypt.

Despite Gaza being strategically crucial to both the Persians and the Macedonians, it was not heavily defended at the time of Alexander's arrival. The garrison, which had no doubt been large in 333, would probably have been denuded by Darius to provide him with extra troops for the ill-fated Battle of Issus. To add to the defenders' difficulties, the garrison was commanded by an otherwise-unattested Persian. The precise name and position of the garrison commander is the subject of some dispute;[155] the text of Curtius reads Betis, more or less the same as the Batis of Arrian, and either of these seems the most likely. Arrian describes the man as a eunuch, although this could be a later invention to make the Persian appear more effeminate. Curtius describes him in entirely neutral terms, stressing his loyalty to Darius and simply noting that he was the commander of the city. Only Josephus specifically describes him as the garrison commander, but the city was small enough that in all likelihood the city governor was also ultimately in command of the garrison.[156] If Batis had indeed been a eunuch then one may imagine Curtius would have mentioned the fact. A eunuch in command of Persian troops would not have been unique; Hermias of Atarneus is also attested to have been a eunuch and ruled in the Troad, whilst Bagoas commanded one third of the entire Persian army during the invasion of Egypt in 343.[157]

Whatever the name and specific designation of the commander, his troops are worthy of note: Arrian describes the defenders as 'Arab mercenaries'. Arab mercenaries are nowhere else attested, although at the Battle of Raphia, Antiochus III raised a force of 10,000 Arab warriors from the Gaza region. Arrian also tells us that they had been preparing for a lengthy siege by stockpiling supplies; they likely would have been expecting Alexander to march south and would have been preparing for most of the nine months it took for Alexander to capture Tyre. We also know that the defenders were well trained and highly motivated.[158]

The city of Gaza was very well located, but its exact situation is the subject of some debate. It would at first appear that the city was built upon an outcrop of rock in the middle of the desert – an island in a sea of sand as it were. The height of the outcrop is the difficulty; the modern mound is some 18-30m above the surrounding desert, but it is likely that at least some of that height would be caused by the accumulated build up of the detritus of civilization over the last twenty-four centuries. We can not know with certainty how high the mound was, but it must have been significant enough to be thought defensible else the city would not have been built there in the first place. The city was also well protected by a crenellated wall that ran the entire length of the circuit of the city. The modern city, which is in the same location, has a circuit of some 3km in total. Batis refused Alexander's order to submit to his rule, believing that the city was virtually impregnable. Its walls were high and strong, the sand around the city was particularly soft and difficult to conduct military operations upon as we will see (although more compact beneath the surface), and the mound was not insignificant. From the outside, the city rose above the level of the surrounding sand and must have looked something like a medieval motte-and-bailey castle with its large central mound. Gaza was evidently well protected, but after the success at Tyre, Alexander would not be easily put off; an assault on Gaza was never in doubt.[159]

It seems likely that Alexander had scouted the city before he arrived as he immediately made camp opposite what he perceived to be the weakest point of the fortifications, and set about rebuilding the siege equipment that he had brought overland from Tyre. The siege engines were evidently capable of being flat-packed for transportation, a clever innovation which would have greatly increased the movement rate of the baggage train. Also immediately upon his arrival he constructed some form of circumvallation around the city, although the details of this will become apparent as we examine the detail of the siege. Behind his lines, and apparently unseen by the defenders, Alexander also began to dig a number of mine shafts in the direction of the city with the intention of undermining and then collapsing the walls. The geology of the area particularly lent itself to this form of siege technique, a technique that Alexander was using here for only the second time as the terrain he had encountered previously on his sieges had been largely rock and entirely unsuitable for sapping. The ground around Gaza was soft sand with no large rock outcroppings, apart from probably the mound upon which the city stood, that would impede the progress of a tunnelling operation. Despite the sand being soft on the surface, it was evidently firm and compacted a few feet below ground, enough that the tunnels did not cave in whilst shafts were being dug. The fact that sapping was begun immediately also tells us that the mound upon which the fortress stood was not of any great size, although still notable for its defensive qualities. If the tell had been as high as it is today, the tunnels would have been too deep beneath the walls for them to have been affected by their collapse once they had been fired.[160]

Once Alexander arrived at the gates of Gaza he made camp and began preparations for the coming siege. His first order was for the construction of what Arrian describes as a turf wall around the city.[161] This turf wall can be seen as a forerunner to the very common Roman practice of circumvallation, something that Alexander was to use whenever he had the opportunity. The most puzzling aspect of this particular offensive fortification is the question of where Alexander got enough turf to construct a circumvallation that must have been in excess of 3km in length, considering that Gaza was located in a desert and surrounded by sand. One possible answer is that the area was perhaps more fertile in the fourth century, and thus there was more turf than there is in that region at present. Upon consideration of the actual events of the siege, this seems extremely unlikely given that we hear of the siege engines sinking into the sand as they were brought up against the walls. If the circumvallation was indeed made of turf, it seems most probable that the turf either came from some distance away, or that Arrian simply made a mistake in using the wrong terminology (i.e. the circumvallation was not made of turf). The latter option seems by far the most probable to me as circumvallations in Arrian's day would probably have been largely made of turf, particularly in Europe; this is probably a simple error by Arrian and nothing more.

Alexander was never a man who was at ease with having men standing idle; at the same time as the circumvallation was being constructed by the troops, his engineers were rebuilding the siege engines that the army had carried from Tyre. The engineers themselves evidently advised Alexander to wait until the bulk of the siege equipment was brought by sea from Tyre, but Alexander ordered them to press on with what they had available, probably the smaller catapults that were more quickly dismantled and more easily transported by cart.

The defensive levee, we are told, was of a size that would allow the catapults and various other siege machines to be at the same level as the city walls:[162]

> The plan of campaign was to enable the siege engines to be brought to bear upon the defences by ringing the town with a raised earthwork up to the level of their base, and mounting the engines upon it.

Arrian is the only one of our sources to stress the size of the walls as being the major difficulty; Curtius chooses to concentrate his attention on the sapping operation, which is only mentioned in passing by Arrian. The reality of the situation was probably that neither ancient source is correct to place stress on only one element of the attack. Throughout his career Alexander would always attack from more than one direction. This was his most frequently used tactic and indeed one of his hallmarks. Both the walls were assaulted directly by catapults, as in Arrian, and the sapping operation was undertaken with equal vigour, as in Curtius. Each historian is simply using a different primary source that placed greater or lesser emphasis upon each of the two elements, ignoring the other almost entirely.[163]

Arrian also tells us that the levee was highest opposite the southern city wall, the area perceived to be the weakest of the entire defensive circuit. When the circumvallation reached the correct height, the siege towers and battering rams were brought up for an assault on the city walls. This is a strong indication that the construction of the circumvallation took a considerable length of time as the siege towers would have been far too cumbersome to have been carried overland, and therefore must have been transported south by ship and dragged the final 4km across the desert. The siege lasted from September to November 332, and we can easily imagine the initial stage of the siege (the construction of the circumvallation, the delivery of the siege towers and the initial sapping operations) as taking up four to six weeks of that time.

There are many problems with the accounts of the early part of the siege. Curtius must be incorrect in stating that the assault on the walls was a diversionary tactic; although this theory would certainly fit well with Alexander's general plan of attacking at various points at once. There would, however, have been no need for a diversion at this time; the point was to collapse the walls, and the more defenders that were in that area when the walls did collapse, the better for Alexander. The attack must have been a serious attempt by Alexander to carry the siege and prevent the work required on the mining operations. The fact that Alexander did not wait for the bulk of his siege engines before commencing sapping operations is either an indication of impatience or a sign that the walls were not as strong as Arrian would have us believe.

The second main problem with the accounts of the first stage of the siege is the circumvallation itself. We are essentially asked to believe that siege towers and battering rams were pulled up to the top of the circumvallation and then down the other side, and that this was seriously seen by Alexander as a viable way to attack the fortifications. It is possible that the mound was only constructed against the southern wall and was not a circumvallation at all.[164] The only supporting evidence for this theory is that Curtius makes no reference to the mound at all during the early narrative of the siege. This is not wholly surprising, however, given that he chose to concentrate his account on the sapping operations. I think this theory can be rejected partly because of this, and partly because it was Alexander's general practice to build a circumvallation where the opportunity presented itself. On the northeast frontier and in India circumvallations are frequently reported, even when the fortress was far less formidable than Gaza. Alexander's primary thinking was likely the defence of his camp from possible sorties as he had experienced at Halicarnassus and Tyre.

Whilst it is possible that the mound was only against one wall, it is contrary to Alexander's strategy at almost every military encounter of his career, that of attacking from multiple directions simultaneously. It would also have been supremely dangerous, as the tunnel would have collapsed the mound as well as the wall. There would have been no way to collapse only a small section of the tunnel. The only possible support for the argument might be to suggest that the mound was built to protect the mining operation from the prying eyes of the defenders, and potentially to attract more of them to that stretch of the wall, so that when it did collapse, more of them would be killed, but this is an untenable argument.

The reality of the situation is almost certainly that the circumvallation was actually built with frequent and regular gaps to allow the siege engines to be dragged along level ground between the raised sections. If this was the case, it also explains how the entire city was surrounded with a mound as high as the city walls in probably only four to six weeks. It seems more plausible that a number, perhaps a large number, of individual mounds were built, upon which the catapults were stationed. This would have looked like a crenellated circumvallation and would be a very clever solution to a potentially difficult problem facing the besiegers of how to get the towers and rams to the walls.

After the initial stages that any siege must undergo, preparation before the assault began. Alexander was ready to commence siege operations proper. We can only imagine the fear and anticipation that the defenders felt at the prospect of the inevitable assault as the circumvallation gained in height, and catapults became a more common site on the highest mounds.

After weeks of preparations, the assault was finally ready to begin; Alexander was about to offer sacrifice to the gods as was the usual practice when a crow flew overhead and dropped a stone upon Alexander's head. Aristander, Alexander's Egyptian seer, interpreted this favourably (again, as was usual) stating that the city would fall, but also offered the warning that Alexander should take care of his own personal safety that day. The story is only of real interest because of what Plutarch reported was the fate of the bird after delivering its payload successfully: the bird became entangled in the cords of a torsion catapult.[165] This gives some indication of the complexity of ancient torsion catapults if nothing else.

Curtius' account is the more interesting, however. He states that the bird landed on the nearest siege tower and that its wings became stuck on the surface, a surface that had been smeared with pitch and sulphur.[166] The question is why would a siege tower be smeared with pitch and sulphur? These chemicals were used in the ancient world as incendiaries, not as flame retardants with we might reasonably expect Alexander to have covered his siege towers, especially after their destruction by fire at Tyre. This exact combination of chemicals had been used by the Spartans against the Plataeans during the siege of that city in 429. Alexander was something of a student of military history and was always one to recycle a good idea. Indeed, this very siege may have formed part of the model for Alexander's attack on Gaza as the Spartans also made use of mounds of earth and built a circumvallation.[167] Along with the siege of Plataea as a precedent, the Peloponnesian War perhaps also provides an explanation for the pitch and sulphur on Alexander's siege towers. Thucydides provides this climactic description of the fall of the Athenian-held fortification at Delium in 424/3:[168]

> The Boeotians took the fort by an engine of the following description. They sawed in two and scooped out a great beam from end to end and fitted it together again like a pipe. They hung by chains a cauldron at one

extremity, with which communicated an iron tube projecting from the beam, and this they brought up on carts to the part of the wall composed of vines and timber and inserted huge bellows into their end of the beam and blew with them. The blast passing closely confined into the cauldron, filled with lighted coals, sulphur and pitch made a great blaze and set fire to the wall and made it impossible for the defenders to remain at their posts. They abandoned their positions and fled; and so the fortifications were captured.

It seems likely to me that Alexander still had fresh in his mind the effect of the Tyrian fire ship against his own siege towers only a few months before. He had seen at first hand how effective fire could be when used correctly and he used the existing precedents to his own advantage at Gaza.

There is only one possible reason that Alexander would cover a siege tower in pitch and sulphur, and that was because he intended it to burn. Alexander wanted the first act of the siege to be a recreation of the fall of Delium and obviate the mines before they were complete. There is no other conceivable explanation for preparing his siege towers to burn at the slightest encouragement. In this act, Alexander shows himself capable of learning the lessons of history, and of trying something innovative.

Despite the incident involving the raven, and Aristander's response, Alexander finally opened the siege proper by ordering the siege engines forward. The opening of the siege turned out to be something of an anti-climax after weeks of build-up; the sand proved to be far too soft and the engines quickly became bogged down in the loose and shifting ground. This hazard should have been anticipated by Alexander's engineers, but evidently was not and this failure left the attackers in a vulnerable position.

It seems probable that Alexander had intended a strong initial assault on the city walls that he hoped would carry the day without the need for a protracted siege as at Tyre and Halicarnassus. With the Macedonians under constant missile bombardment from the defenders, however, and unable to respond in kind because of the difficulties of bringing enough engines close to the walls, Alexander changed his strategy and evidently held back the bulk of the quality troops.[169] At the same time as holding back these quality troops, those who were in the forefront of the assault were ordered to withdraw and, wherever possible, to rescue the beached siege engines. As the Macedonians were struggling to execute the order for withdrawal, whilst also attempting to extricate their siege equipment from the desert sands, Batis ordered a sortie from the city, just as Memnon and the Tyrians had done before him.

Alexander's adaptability during this siege is quite brilliant and is hinted at in Arrian. Alexander quickly realized that his initial assault would fail because of the siege engines becoming bogged down, and that he would suffer heavy losses if he continued the siege without them. His change of strategy was essentially twofold: he seemingly expected, or anticipated, a counter-attack from Batis when the defenders saw the difficulties that the Macedonians were in. This form of sortie was a well-practised defensive tactic and one that Alexander had seen several times during his sieges to date. If Batis was to undertake a sortie, Alexander wanted to ensure that his troops were ready to launch their own counter-attack against them and catch them unprepared as the Gazans would no doubt be concentrating on the destruction of the siege engines. Alexander would not be caught unprepared again as he had been at Halicarnassus. The second element was that if Batis did not counter-attack, Alexander left enough forward troops to drag the siege engines to safety, out of missile range of the walls. This rapid evolution of strategy essentially saw Alexander failing in his initial plan but immediately devising a method of attempting to lure the defenders into a hastily prepared trap that would recover the difficult situation he found himself in. This would be entirely consistent with Alexander's repeated strategy of always fighting battles on terrain of his choosing, even during a siege as here.

If a sortie was indeed what Alexander was expecting after his initial reverse, then he was not to be disappointed. Arrian tells us:[170]

> Before long, however, the defenders of the town made a sortie in strength; the Arab troops endeavoured to set fire to the siege engines, and the heavy attacks with missile weapons delivered from their commanding position almost succeeded in thrusting the Macedonians back down the earthwork they had raised.

After what Curtius described as something of an assassination attempt on the part of one of the Arab mercenaries, Alexander organized the hypaspists and attacked the Arabs who had sortied from the town.[171] Alexander's counter-attack was delivered with his usual use of tactical skill and the application of overwhelming force at exactly the correct location, and he succeeded in driving back the Arabs with heavy losses to them. During this counter-attack against the Arab mercenaries, and counter to the advice of Aristander who had warned Alexander to take care after the incident with the crow, Alexander was struck by a bolt from an arrow-throwing catapult stationed upon the walls. The bolt penetrated his shield and cuirass and struck him in the shoulder. The wound was grievous, and Alexander was carried from the field, not for the last time during his career. The defenders evidently believed that they had slain the Macedonian king, and began celebrating a great victory.[172]

Alexander's wound was serious, and seems to have taken him several weeks to recover as there appears to have been a significant pause in the siege at this juncture. The time was not wasted, however. Further preparations were undertaken for the final stages, the mounds that formed the circumvallation were strengthened and raised and the engineers redoubled their efforts on the mines, as well as the bulk of the artillery having arrived by sea from Tyre.[173] Curtius suggests that Alexander was adopting a new tactic at this point, but it seems more reasonable to suggest that he was building upon the tactic that he had already decided upon.

Some modern historians have believed the circumvallation mounds to have been rather low, but this almost certainly underestimated the amount of earth 30–40,000 men could move by hand in a couple of weeks. Arrian went the other way and claimed the circumvallation mounds were up to c.76m high, but the modern mound upon which the city sits is only c.30m high and Arrian surely makes a mistake in his interpretation of his sources.[174]

After what we can only describe as a failure to capture the city as Alexander had hoped, albeit having turned the initial mistake into a minor tactical victory in driving off the Arabs with heavy losses, Alexander was in much the same position as he had been in prior to the aborted assault. After a trip of apparently several weeks, the heavy artillery pieces and the siege towers that had been instrumental in the capture of Tyre finally arrived after having been transported first by boat and then dragged across the desert to the Macedonian camp; Arrian goes on to say:[175]

> The artillery was assembled, mounted on the earthwork, and brought into action. Long stretches of the wall suffered damage, saps were dug at various points, the earth removed unobserved by the enemy, until in many places the wall, having nothing to support it, collapsed and fell.

Once Alexander had recovered from his wound, and once the mines and machines were in place, the final stage of the siege began. The wooden supports in the mines were set ablaze, the catapults began their volleys and the rams were moved up against the walls. In relatively short order the mines collapsed, bringing several stretches of the walls down with them.[1765]

Much as in every siege, once a gap appeared in the wall Alexander began a concerted assault, although evidently not with his crack troops. Initially, there was an artillery and missile barrage on the walls close to the toppled section to soften up the defenders for the final assault. After this barrage, Alexander made the first assault; this evidently made some progress, but the Arab mercenaries were fighting for their lives and managed to repulse the Macedonians' first assault. Alexander's sub-commanders gathered together their men for a second mighty assault, and again the Arab defenders, who by now would have been significantly outnumbered, fought off the Macedonians and forced a second withdrawal. A third attempt by the Macedonians met with the same fate, but by this time the Arab defenders would have been exhausted and seriously overmatched. The Macedonians appear to have wasted no time in organizing a fourth assault, this time by the elite hypaspists and the heavy infantry:[177]

> Alexander brought into action the main body of the heavy infantry on all sides of the town, the wall, already under-mined, was battered down or widely breached where artillery had already done its work, so that it was now an easy matter to get ladders on to the shattered defences, and thus force an entry.

Once the ladders were in position, or troops were standing opposite a breach in the wall, the attackers apparently vied with each other to be the first to enter the city and claim their prize. The first man into the city was an otherwise unknown Neoptolemus, a member of the Companion Cavalry who must surely have been fighting on foot at this point. Alexander really was, it seems, using his elite troops, whatever their usual designation. These elite troops succeeded where earlier assaults had failed; the result of the Macedonians gaining access to the city was all too predictable. Terrible slaughter and looting ensued until every appetite of the invaders was sated.

The story found in Curtius,[178] although perhaps revealingly not Arrian, of Batis being dragged behind Alexander's chariot, whilst still alive, around the circuit of the city is an intriguing one:

> Alexander's anger turned to fury, his recent successes already suggesting to his mind foreign modes of behaviour. Thongs were passed through Betis' ankles while he still breathed, and he was tied to a chariot. Then Alexander's horses dragged him around the city while the king gloated at having followed the example of his ancestor Achilles in punishing his enemy.

The Homeric original to the story presents Achilles dragging Hector's *corpse* behind his chariot, but here Batis is still alive; the incident here seems unusual in the context of Homer but not unbelievable.[179] The most we can say is that such an act would have appealed to Alexander's sense of kinship with Achilles. The absence of this story from our other sources is puzzling, except to say that incidents that a flattering source may have considered unworthy of Alexander could easily have been omitted.

The mad dash that was the end of the siege is seemingly uncharacteristic of the Macedonians. During the final stages, however, when booty was there for the taking and the Macedonians were about to fall upon the civilian population, with all of the horrors that entailed, it was probably all but impossible for Alexander to maintain any kind of discipline, as we saw at Thebes. Perhaps the real surprise is that some cities were left standing after being taken by force by the Macedonians (or indeed by any ancient army).

As a result of its capture the city suffered badly, but had recovered enough that by 315 it was able to attempt a resistance to Antigonus. The inhabitants of the city were not so lucky; the women and children being sold into slavery and most of the male defenders were slaughtered in the final assault.[180] As at Thebes before it, this act evidently raised considerable sums for the Macedonian coffers, although the money was not a prime motivating factor by 331. Alexander soon after sent his former tutor 500 talents of frankincense and 100 talents of myrrh.

The siege of Gaza could be described as a relatively straightforward affair; the fortress was not built on a precipitous outcropping of rock as at Pir-Sar, nor was it built in another topographically defensible location such as the island city of Tyre. Nevertheless, Gaza was strongly fortified and on a rocky outcrop and was defended by a motivated and extremely capable force of around 10,000 Arab mercenaries, and was therefore not an easy siege; the three month duration is testimony to that. The siege of Gaza also presents us with a situation virtually unique in Alexander's career, a city built on sand or soft rock, rather than hard granite-like rock. This topography allowed Alexander to perform sapping operations that we only see one other time during Alexander's early career. These sapping operations were ultimately a fundamental part of the fall of the city. As at Tyre a few months earlier, Alexander was presented with a situation that required a novel solution, and he was not found wanting. Along with this relatively new tactic, we see old ideas employed to great effect. As noted several times, Alexander's key tactic was always to attack from multiple directions simultaneously. At Gaza he achieves this by employing what could be called an interrupted circumvallation with artillery pieces located on the various mounds around the circuit, along with the use of rams and siege towers in the intervening gaps (and of course ladders were possible). Complementing the siege engines was the final ingenious element of the mining operations. Gaza, like Tyre before it, shows Alexander to be a commander who was highly capable of creating innovative tactics when the need arose, or the situation allowed for it.

After the successful capture of Gaza, Alexander continued southwest into Egypt to complete the strategy that he had set out at Halicarnassus: that of reducing the Persian fleet by capturing its naval bases and denying it safe haven. In reality, the strategy was now moot as Alexander was effectively in control of the Persian fleet after the desertions to his banner during the siege of Tyre and afterwards. Alexander's real intention in capturing Egypt was to prevent the possibility of leaving potentially-hostile territory in his rear as he was about to advance into the Persian heartlands, but also to secure the breadbasket of Egypt. Alexander always took great care over logistics as demonstrated by the almost total lack of supply difficulties noted in the sources during his career, with the obvious exception of the Gedrosian Desert disaster. Alexander also had a yearning (*pothos*) to visit the oracle at Siwah, although when he first developed this is unclear and it may not have been a significant motivation for the invasion, perhaps only occurring while in Egypt.

Alexander set out for Egypt soon after the capture of Gaza was complete, leaving the usual numbers of troops as a garrison with the intention of repairing the city and maintaining it as it always had been, a sentinel guarding the entry (or exit in the case of revolt) to Egypt. The siege engines, so destructive and instrumental in the previous twelve months, would have been dismantled for transport and probably sent back to Tyre to await Alexander's return from Egypt and the campaign into the Persian heartlands. They likely would not have accompanied Alexander as he would not have expected resistance, and their presence in the baggage train would have slowed him down significantly. Alexander's intelligence network would no doubt have told him that Egypt was unlikely to resist his advance, and would see him as a liberator from Persian despotism. This proved correct and the Macedonians were welcomed, Alexander being recognized as Pharaoh. The implicit assumption of divinity that went along with this status would no doubt have particularly pleased the king.

After a brief stay, which is of historical but no military interest, Alexander retraced his steps, marching on Tyre for a second time. The rebuilding work was in full swing, but Alexander had evidently ordered the mole to be left in position, and it is still visible today as the causeway connecting the former island to the mainland.

Alexander now had no reason to delay the final showdown with his Persian rival any longer: the hunt for Darius was now on. Alexander marched northeast into the heartland of Persia. After a stunning victory at Gaugamela in 331 (analyzed in my forthcoming volume *The Field Campaigns of Alexander the Great*), Alexander found himself lord of Asia, the new Great King. Alexander then spent time mopping up the great cities of the Persian heartlands, none of whom offered resistance. The only campaign of note was the forcing of the Persian Gates. Although, not technically a siege, it should be examined because it does contain many similarities.

Persian Gates

After a brief delay sacking Uxii villages, Alexander divided his forces, as was to become his usual practice as he entered this new region. The mercenary and allied troops, together with the baggage train, were left under the command of Parmenio to travel towards Persepolis via what Arrian describes as the 'carriage road'. Although this was the main route to Persepolis, it was not the quickest; Alexander chose the direct but less-used route over the mountains, and he made good time as the slowest elements of the army had been left behind with Parmenio.

Ariobarzanes had taken up a defensive position in the pass known as the Persian Gates, and had taken the time to prepare his position well. He had built a wall across the narrow pass and had men stationed on the heights to either side. Alexander advanced upon the gates slowly and with extreme caution, taking five days to travel the final 30km, evidently aware of the dangers and expecting an attack of some kind.[181] Alexander's first response upon seeing the wall shows an uncharacteristic lack of style, imagination, thought or preparation. Almost immediately, he launched a frontal assault. It could be that he attempted the same tactic as had worked against the Uxii previously, to terrify them into retreat without the need for battle. Alexander was not facing Uxii villagers, however, but Persian infantry. Whilst the Persians did not possess first-class infantrymen, they certainly had greater discipline than the Uxii, and they had the advantage of a well-prepared defensive position; the Persians held their ground. The frontal assault was an unmitigated disaster. Missiles rained down upon the attackers from the heights to either side, as well as from those defending the wall. The Macedonians quickly fell back in disorder, leaving behind their dead in the pass.[182]One can only imagine the fury that Alexander must have felt at this humiliation. Defeat was extremely rare in Alexander's career, but the blame here lies squarely upon his shoulders. Even within this fury Alexander was evidently rational enough, or had good enough counsel, to realize that a further frontal assault would not fare any better, and a different strategy must be found. Despite the failure of the assault, Alexander had evidently at least managed to engage the enemy directly as he had managed to capture a small number of the defenders. These were now interrogated (or perhaps local hill farmers were questioned). After this interrogation, a secondary path was revealed – the parallels with Thermopylae hardly need mentioning.

Alexander was informed by the prisoners that the pass was narrow and difficult to traverse. Upon hearing this, he instructed Craterus to remain behind with his own *taxis* and that of Meleager, along with some archers and cavalry, whilst he would set off along the mountain pass. Craterus was instructed to launch a further frontal assault only when they were sure that Alexander was behind the Persians. Arrian claims the remainder of the troops travelled with Alexander through the pass.

Alexander waited for the cover of darkness, and then set off for the alternative route. After a night march of around 20km, Alexander took the decision to divide his forces further. He took with him one *taxis* of heavy infantry, the Agrianians and archers, along with the Royal *ile* of Companions and one double squadron of cavalry.[183] With these troops Alexander turned and moved towards the pass. The remaining troops were probably ordered to bridge the Araxes River that would need to be crossed in order to gain access to central Persia.[184] These troops probably were not used as a third column against the defenders, as the passes were narrow and large numbers of troops were already operating with difficulty in the area. The idea of a three-pronged attack is attractive, but if the pass and the terrain was as difficult as we are led to believe, then I think it is more plausible that Alexander realized that he had taken too many troops with him through the pass as it was. His intention, therefore, was to reduce the numbers that would be involved in the final assault to only the elite. Whatever the purpose of Amyntas' detachment, it is certain that Alexander led the assault in person.

The action at the gates probably occurred over two consecutive nights, with Alexander showing considerable caution in avoiding the Persian scouting parties that were no doubt at work in the area. Once he was ready for the final assault, he came down upon the defenders from the northeast destroying two forward fortifications and falling upon the wall.[185] The attack was signalled by the use of a *salpinx*, a trumpet-like instrument, which acted as the signal for Craterus to attack down the gorge. The Persians were caught totally by surprise by the two-pronged attack. There were few places to run or hide for the Persians, although Ariobarzanes and a small group of horsemen and infantry did manage an escape. Ariobarzanes fled to Persepolis where he was refused entry; he died in an engagement with the advancing Macedonians shortly afterwards, fighting the foreign conqueror to the last.[186]

In this capture of another fortified position, hardly lasting long enough to warrant the term 'siege', Alexander once again shows a genius for rapid and silent movements of large bodies of men in order to maintain the element of surprise. We also see Alexander, once again, using the two-pronged approach of attacking the enemy from more than one direction. This has to be balanced, however, against Alexander's serious lack of judgement at the initial assault; to sacrifice men so needlessly when his usual flanking tactic was so readily available (once the pass had been identified) is puzzling. We can only assume that he felt the defenders would retreat immediately upon seeing his advance, as the Uxians had done.

After forcing the Persian Gates, Alexander made for Ecbatana. Before heading off into what would become the northeast frontier of his new empire, Alexander spent some time reorganizing his army and dealing with some internal difficulties (for example, the murders of Philotas and Parmenio). Up to this point in the campaign Alexander had been in territory that was foreign but not unknown to him, as Greeks had been trading and working in the western Persian Empire for generations; the region he was about to enter was a different story, however.

Chapter 6

The Northeast Frontier: 330–327

The Bactrian campaign began slowly, with Alexander wintering his troops (330/29) in the southern Helmand province, which was, in terms of food supply to the eastern satrapies, as Egypt was to the west. After securing Hyrcania, a little known region between Ecbatana and Bactria, Alexander marched on the province of Bactria. Ancient Bactria was as far removed, topographically and socially, from the Greek world as one can imagine. The soaring mountains of the Hindu Kush and the Pamir ranges surrounded Bactria on three sides. The west to northwest was bordered by the deserts of modern Turkestan, through which runs the Oxus River (Amu Darya) on its way to the Aral Sea. This was terrain that was entirely alien to Alexander, and indeed any Greek. No longer would Alexander be facing large armies in massive set-piece battles. From this time forward, at least until he reached India, he would be facing an entirely-new form of combat: that of guerrilla warfare. Alexander would now face small-scale ambushes and rapid strikes against his forces. He faced an enemy that knew it could not defeat him in battle, and was wise enough not to try. The Bactrians were well aware of their own strengths, and had had enough reports from the western satrapies as to be well aware of Alexander's too, and constantly attempted to pick and choose their battles in order to maximize their own strengths and minimize their weaknesses. The natives, probably over centuries of warfare, had devised an alternative means of fighting that used the very land of Bactria to its fullest advantage.

The initial phase of the campaigns in Bactria and Sogdiana are fascinating as well as complex, and will be examined in *The Field Campaigns of Alexander the Great*; but they do not see Alexander conducting typical siege operations and so are not relevant here. After Gaza in 332, the first siege Alexander was able to conduct was that of the Sogdian Rock, probably in the summer of 328, a gap of almost four years.

Sogdian Rock/ Rock of Arimazes

Alexander's apparent strategy of militarizing the Sogdian frontier culminated with the construction of a series of garrison settlements in what is now called Tadzhikistan. Alexander moved east through the region and towards the Hissar Range separating east and west Sogdiana, occupying strongholds as he went, but with only minor resistance until he reached the Sogdian Rock, or as it was sometimes known, the Rock of Arimazes, probably in the summer of 328.[187] The rock was some 6,000m high and 30km in circumference. The fortress boasted sheer cliffs on all sides, and Oxyartes evidently felt the fortress was impregnable as he had sent his family to the rock for their own safety. Arrian described the Sogdian Rock as the 'last stronghold in Sogdiana'. The Sogdian Rock was heavily defended: a total of 30,000 natives are reported to have taken refuge within its walls.[188] The fortress was well stocked with food, and there was enough snow on the heights that could easily be converted into drinking water. Therefore the fortress was unlikely to be starved into submission.

Alexander would have been travelling through this most difficult terrain without his siege train; this was partly because of the difficulty of traversing these mountain passes, partly because Alexander had an overwhelming need for rapidity of movement and partly because he simply had not needed it for some years, as already noted. Alexander was now faced with a potentially extremely difficult siege without any siege engines, and with a lack of trees in the region, which seriously limited the ability of his engineers to construct more. The Sogdian Rock also could not be subjected to a simple frontal assault as the mountain upon which it stood was inaccessible to any significant number of troops; the path that led to it was narrow and not suitable for a frontal assault. Curtius tells us that Alexander seriously considered abandoning the siege before it even began as he apparently saw no obvious way of successfully carrying the Rock. It was only his longing (*pothos*) that again overcame him, as it did at numerous occasions during his career. Even with this ephemeral *pothos*, Alexander was still faced with the all-too-practical problem of how to assault the fortress. Alexander began by trying to avoid having to assault the citadel and attempted diplomacy. He sent Cophes, the son of Artabazus, to urge the natives to abandon the Rock and to surrender to Alexander. If they were to do this they were offered the opportunity to return to their homelands unmolested. Their response was simply to laugh in the face of Alexander's representative. Arimazes, the commander of the Rock, was so confident in his position that, along with a number of far more insulting barbs, he asked Cophes if the Macedonians had brought flying troops with them, for this was the only way they could reach the fortress. Alexander was so enraged by this lack of respect that any thoughts of abandoning the siege were now gone. Arimazes' words were ill advised as this barb appears to have given Alexander perhaps the kernel of an idea that he was to put into action the following night.

Alexander ordered his senior commanders to each have 300 men brought before him; these were to be only the fittest and most agile of the entire army. When these men had been gathered together, Alexander addressed the miniature assembly telling the troops that he wanted volunteers to climb the mountain upon which stood the fortress, a climb that was difficult enough, but was to be conducted under cover of night and in the extreme cold suggested by the snow on the mountain and its approaches. The prize for volunteers was a king's ransom: the first to the top was to receive ten talents, the second nine talents, etc. We do not know what those who did not finish in the top ten were to receive – perhaps nothing at all. Arrian tells us 'the men were keen enough already, but this proclamation was an added spur'.[189] In all, 300 men volunteered, Curtius telling us they were particularly tough herdsmen from the Macedonian uplands, men who also had distinguished themselves as mountaineers in earlier sieges – sieges that apparently did not warrant great description by any source but probably ones conducted earlier in the Bactrian and Sogdian campaigns.

Alexander had developed a cunning and daring ruse by which he hoped to capture the Rock, a ruse that would rely for its success on stealth and perfect timing. Probably late afternoon of the night that the climb was due to commence, Alexander gathered together the 300 brave, yet slightly foolhardy, warriors warriors and explained to them what he required of them and how he planned to carry the siege. Alexander told the men:[190]

> You will find a way up if you use your skill in searching for tracks that lead to the top. Nature has set nothing so high that it cannot be surmounted by courage. It is by using methods of which others have despaired that we have Asia in our power. Get to the top. When you have reached it, give me a signal with pieces of white cloth and I shall advance troops to divert the enemy's attention from you to us.

They were evidently not put off by the high degree of personal danger involved in the climb, and apparently greatly inspired by Alexander's words. The mountaineers faced an extremely difficult climb made all the more troublesome by the fact that it would have to be conducted at night to avoid any chance of the defenders realizing what was happening if the ruse that Alexander had planned was to be successful. The mountaineers equipped themselves with:[191]

> Small iron tent-pegs, which they proposed to drive into the snow, where it was frozen hard, or into any bit of bare earth they might come across, and they had attached to the pegs strong flaxen lines.

Improvised pitons and rope are hardly ideal preparations for a difficult night time ascent of a mountain, but with only this equipment, they waited for nightfall and then began to climb. Arian tells us that the steepest and most precipitous face was chosen because this was the least likely to be guarded, although Curtius tells us the opposite, that they climbed the least difficult face. Either way, they were not likely to have been spotted at night even if there were regular patrols at the summit of the mountain.

The ascent began at second watch after Alexander had personally ridden around the mountain to determine the most advantageous place to climb. Along with their climbing equipment the mountaineers took only two days' rations and their swords and spears, probably strapped to their backs to allow both hands to be kept free. The climb started well:[192]

> They started out on foot, but then they reached the sheer parts. Here some pulled themselves up by grasping protruding rocks with their hands; others climbed by means of ropes with sliding knots which they threw ahead of themselves; others again used the pins, wedging them between rocks to serve as steps on which they could get a footing from time to time.

Quickly the climb became far more difficult, however; the mountain became ever steeper and the rock face increasingly sheer. The rate of climb slowed significantly and it surely must have taken place over two nights; a 6,000m climb at night with no breathing apparatus stretches credulity too far to be believable. Curtius goes on to tell us that:[193]

> It was truly pitiful to see men who had been deceived by an unsure footing plunge headlong, and such a calamity overtaking another served to warn the rest that the same fate would soon be theirs.

After a difficult night spent on the mountain, the remaining mountaineers would have hidden in any cave or crevasse that they could to avoid detection by the defenders, and the exposure of the ruse. The tired and cold men would have taken what rest they could during the long day, awaiting nightfall once more so that they could complete their climb. When night did finally arrive they crawled out of their hiding places and began to climb once more. They reached the summit before dawn the following day and waited for the sun to rise as Alexander had instructed.

At dawn they signalled Alexander that they had arrived safely and were in position above the defenders. Alexander saw the signal and moved the army to the narrow path leading to the fortress, as previously arranged, and sent a herald to speak to the defenders. Once the army was in position, the defenders presumably also having moved to the gate to see what was going on, the mountaineers began to shout and wave their weapons around in the early morning light. The herald declared that Alexander had indeed found flying men, and that nobody and nothing could stand in his way; surrender was their only hope. The morale of the defenders, and the arrogance of Arimazes, disintegrated almost instantly: the Rock surrendered to Alexander without further loss of life.[194]

In order to complete their surrender, and probably on the orders of Alexander, Arimazes came to Alexander's camp in person, along with some of his relatives and the leading citizens within the fortress. Alexander was apparently still furious at the arrogance displayed to him and his herald by Arimazes upon his initial offer of a peaceful solution, and he now had his opportunity to exact revenge. Alexander first ordered those who had come into his camp to be whipped and then crucified at the foot of the Rock that was their home. The remainder of the citizens and defenders were given as gifts to the peoples of the newly-founded cities in the region, and the citadel was given to Artabazus, along with the territory that it commanded.

Both Arrian and Curtius confirm that thirty-two men died during the arduous climb. An attrition rate of only ten per cent seems rather low for such a difficult and dangerous task.[195] At the outset of the siege we can assume that Alexander would have gladly sacrificed thirty-two men (and the fifty-five talents it would have cost him as reward to the first ten mountaineers) to capture such a fortress. The loss of life would have been far worse if an actual assault was forced upon the Macedonians.

In the capture of this mountain-top fortress, Alexander once again showed himself capable of analyzing a seemingly impossible situation and formulating a winning strategy. We also see an example of Alexander taking a calculated risk, that the defenders would surrender at the sight of his flying men, rather than attack the mountaineers whom they surely outnumbered by at least twenty to one, and he was again proved correct; Alexander was nothing if not lucky throughout his career.

Rock of Chorienes/Rock of Sisimithres

After a lengthy delay, which consisted of only minor campaigning in Maracanda, and culminated in the murder of Black Cleitus, autumn was suddenly upon the Macedonians. Before the year's end, however, one final campaign awaited Alexander. From Maracanda, Alexander marched south to eliminate a group of Bactrian rebels who were based in the city of Xenippa, the exact location of which still remains unknown. No details are known about the campaign, other than its successful nature. We can probably draw the conclusion, however, that the campaign was a relatively minor affair as it is largely ignored by all of the sources. Alexander then moved to what would become his winter quarters in Nautaca, probably located between Maracanda and the Oxus River.[196] Nautaca was the last refuge of the rebels commanded by Sisimithres (although Arrian calls him Chorienes, probably a corruption of Sisimithres). These Alexander forced into submission too as the last military action of 328.

For his final stand, Sisimithres was firmly ensconced in yet another seemingly impregnable citadel. The fortress was, like the Sogdian Rock, located on the peak of a large hill, or perhaps a small mountain. The hill was partially surrounded by a deep ravine and was thus inaccessible to a direct assault. The ravine was also wide enough that Alexander's siege engines simply could not directly engage the walls; they could not get close enough. This fortress was, again, well stocked with food and water sufficient to support the defenders during a lengthy siege.

The ravine, combined with its torrent of water from the plateau above, meant that the fortress was naturally well defended. This was coupled with the circuit of well-built stone walls to present Alexander with another difficult siege. Arrian has the ravine encircle the Rock, but this cannot be so as the torrent of water in it was essentially a river and therefore surely must have led somewhere beyond the fortress, the fortress surrounded on three sides by the river is more likely. Arrian's description appears to be something of a stock description, or else he is confusing two sources who gave slightly different descriptions; we must remember that the sources we have are extremely unlikely to have personally viewed this region of the empire.[197]

As usual, Alexander did not allow a natural barrier, however seemingly formidable, to stand against him. Alexander's tactics are often brilliantly subtle with numerous sub-strategies that feed off the primary; occasionally, however, his methods were brutally direct. During this siege, Alexander used the precedent first set at Tyre; he set about building a causeway across the chasm. The causeway was a marvellous feat of engineering that is almost always underappreciated by modern historians. It consisted of a series of interlocking stakes that were cantilevered over the narrowest point of the gorge.[198] The descent to the bottom of the deep gorge to lay the wooden foundations and to drive the huge wooden stakes into position must have been an extremely hazardous task about which we hear little. Whilst in the gorge, Alexander's engineers also had to take care to firmly secure the base of the causeway against being swept away by the fast-flowing waters within the gorge. As during the later siege of Aornus the following year, Alexander supervised the work personally, and split his men into two shifts, day and night. Progress was slower than it was to be at Aornus, where the men constructed a stade-long stretch in a single day; access was more limited on this occasion.

The siege shows many similarities with the earlier siege of Tyre, similarities that perhaps have been deliberately exaggerated for effect. We are, as at Tyre, presented with the picture of the defenders treating the construction of the causeway as something of a joke, perhaps not believing that such a construction was even possible. This is exactly the reaction of the Tyrians until they saw the causeway getting ever closer to their island. As the causeway was developing, probably being built from the bottom of the gorge upwards, rather than from one side to the other, the defenders began to try to disrupt the construction teams by firing arrows upon them. This proved to be ineffective partially because of the distances involved, and partly because Alexander had learned the lessons of earlier siege operations and had deployed portable and moveable *abates* to protect the construction crews.

The work was difficult and therefore proceeded slowly; perversely this probably worked to Alexander's advantage, however. As the causeway grew at a slow but dreadfully-inevitable rate, Sisimithres had plenty of time to become increasingly worried for his position and his fortress. Sisimithres had become aware, probably through previous attempts at diplomacy that Oxyartes was with Alexander's host. Oxyartes was a neighbour and fellow tribesman of Sisimithres, now allied with Alexander. He was evidently a man trusted by the defenders. Sisimithres requested, via a herald, that Oxyartes be allowed to approach and enter the citadel so that they may converse regarding the current situation. Alexander allowed the parlay, hoping that Oxyartes could persuade the defenders of the wisdom of surrender, and the inevitability of death or slavery if they did not. In order to put continued pressure upon the defenders, especially during the talks:[199]

> Siege towers were brought forward and a barrage of missiles flashed from the siege engines.

This attempt at a diplomatic solution evidently came rather late in proceedings; if the siege towers were able to get close enough to the walls to launch a volley then they must have been on the causeway, which must, therefore, have been partially complete. The top of the causeway would probably have been a wicker flooring that would support the earth and wood that would form the walkway across the ravine.

Oxyartes evidently tried to persuade Sisimithres that Alexander was an honourable man, citing himself as evidence that capitulation to the conqueror meant survival and prosperity. Sisimithres had evidently heard stories of Alexander's previous successful operations against seemingly-impregnable fortresses, and was becoming increasingly concerned for the safety of his position, and so he decided to trust the word of Oxyartes. He sent Oxyartes back to the Macedonian camp with an offer of his surrender; this Alexander accepted and returned him to his throne with a hint that his kingdom would expand if he proved his loyalty. Alexander's price was a surprisingly Macedonian one: Sisimithres' two sons were to accompany Alexander on his future conquests, essentially acting as hostages against their father's good behaviour; this is something that was a regular tradition in Macedonian history.

During this brief but, from an engineering perspective, extremely interesting siege, Alexander showed himself capable of learning difficult lessons from earlier sieges, specifically Tyre. At Tyre, Alexander only adopted defensive measures after suffering losses to ship-borne missile weapons. Hides were placed at the leading edge of the bridge to protect the builders and engineers from projectile weapons fired by the defenders.[200] The defenders did not have the same will to resist as did the Tyrians, and at this display of siegecraft they surrendered before a final assault could be started against the defences proper. The Rock's vast stores of provisions were enough to winter the Macedonian army; yet again Alexander avoided any serious logistical issues.

Upon the successful completion of the siege, winter was soon to be upon the Macedonians. Alexander made for Nautaca where he would winter the troops and await the new campaigning season of 327. The difficulties that Alexander had faced in Bactria and Sogdiana meant that he could not simply leave the region without the reasonable expectation that rebellion would occur once again as soon as he was too far away to respond quickly, and he could not allow the northeast frontier to delay his advance into India. With hindsight, this is a similar difficulty to that encountered in northern Greece, and his response was similar. During the Battles of Issus and Gaugamela, Alexander had been greatly impressed by the quality of the troops that the region had supplied to Darius (particularly the cavalry), and indeed in those he had faced in the recent rebellion. Alexander had a constant need for fresh, high-quality troops, and he also came to realize that reinforcements were drying up from Macedonia. With these factors in mind Alexander began a recruiting program that winter that he hoped would eliminate these long-term recruitment problems. This now-famous training program saw Alexander recruit (or more likely conscript) 30,000 Persian youths into the army. These were to be trained and equipped in the Macedonian-style, and educated in Macedonian tactics, essentially making them replacements for the *pezhetairoi*.[201] The policy did not stop with infantry, however; significant numbers of native cavalry were also enlisted. Alexander would have been especially impressed by these during the two earlier set-piece battles, and his need for quality cavalry was always greatest as these were the strike force of the whole army.

This recruitment drive had a twofold effect. Firstly, it strengthened the Macedonian field army considerably in anticipation of the coming Indian campaign; secondly, and perhaps more importantly, it removed significant numbers of potentially rebellious troops from Sogdiana and Bactria. This is exactly what Alexander had done in the Balkans in 335 when he conscripted thousands of Thracians, Odrysians, Triballians etc. It was also the general policy of the Roman Empire to station auxiliary troops as far as possible from their homelands.

Chapter 7

India and the Journey to Babylon: 327-323

In the spring of 327, after a brief yet busy two-month winter stay in Nautaca, Alexander set off south for Bactra where he paused, leaving behind three *taxeis* of *pezhetairoi* with Craterus in command to complete the reduction of the region, before continuing south to rendezvous with Alexander in India. It is apparent that Alexander had been contemplating an Indian campaign for some time, at least since summer the previous year, and almost certainly long before that.[202] Alexander's constant desire, or more likely need, for exploration, discovery and conquest meant that he could never have refused the opportunity that India presented.

The army that marched out of Bactria with Alexander was around 50,000 strong, hardly more than had fought at Gaugamela. The relative proportion of the Macedonian contingent had been reduced, however, as there had been no documented reinforcements from Macedonia for almost four years, and the strain was starting to show. We do know of a large influx of reinforcements from Greece, but these had been left behind in Bactria and Sogdiana (apparently reluctantly given their future rebellions and attempts to get home) to ensure that there were no further difficulties in that region. The organization of the army had also changed in order to make it more mobile and able to respond to changing circumstances: the *pezhetairoi* had all but abandoned the *sarissa*; its use is not recorded again in the sources (interestingly, apart from a few minor occasions, the only time we know positively that the *sarissa* was used was at Gaugamela). The *prodromoi* had also been merged with the Companion Cavalry, probably a sign of seriously reduced numbers. This is also a likely proof that they were Macedonian in origin, rather than Balkan, as is sometimes assumed. Orientals also started to be introduced into the ranks of the Companion Cavalry for the first time, again indicating declining numbers of Macedonians available to Alexander. A new officer class had also emerged in Sogdiana, partly through the constant desire to remove 'Philip's men' from the command structure and replace them with his own. This policy had seen the removal of men like Parmenio, Philotas and Cleitus. The new officer cadre consisted of Alexander's childhood friends, men he believed he could trust intimately: the likes of Hephaestion, Ptolemy and Perdiccas.[203]

Ten days march south from Bactra took the army back across the Hindu Kush Mountains and into Parapamisadae. From there they advanced down the Cophen River Valley (now called the Kabul River Valley) towards the plains of the Indus and the satrapy of Bajaur.[204] After what we can only assume would have been a difficult and time consuming crossing of the Hindu Kush, given the narrow passes and the baggage train that the army carried, Alexander divided the army into two columns, as had become the general policy. The first column was commanded by Hephaestion and Perdiccas, and consisted of three *taxeis* of heavy infantry (those of Gorgias, Cleitus the White and Meleager), half the Companion Cavalry and all of the mercenary cavalry, a total of around 6-7,000 men.[205] This column was instructed to secure the main road into India, no simple task. The remainder of the army, commanded by Alexander, marched into the mountainous terrain north of the Kabul River, the regions of Bajaur and Swat, continuing the brutal campaign that he had started in Sogdiana; Alexander's desire to punish the natives had evidently not yet been sated.[206] This is also likely an indication that Alexander did not have the same geographical distinction between Bactria, Sogdiana and India that we do today. He may have seen these people as being essentially the same as those he had been campaigning against previously and in need of subjugation.

At first glance this campaign looks punitive and brutal, but it was vital in order to protect his lines of supply and communication down the Kabul River Valley from the central Persian satrapies. Alexander saw all of the inhabitants of the region as his subjects, given his status as the Great King, and any resistance was a direct challenge to his rule, and any challenge was increasingly met with bloody and brutal repression.[207] Alexander's campaign to the north of the Kabul River began with an assault on an anonymous local town. The inhabitants had retired to their mountain stronghold and had made ready to resist Alexander. Why they chose resistance we do not know, but the previous Persian presence in this region was probably very mild and they would have been almost entirely autonomous before the arrival of the Macedonians. In the initial assault against the fortification, Alexander was slightly wounded by an arrow to the shoulder. This, coupled with his desire to make an example of them, led directly to a massacre of the defenders, something that was becoming all too familiar as Alexander met increased resistance with absolute repression.[208] There is little doubt that this act was a deliberate policy designed to terrify the native population into submission in much the same way as the Mongols were to do during their conquest of Central Asia. Curtius tells us that even before the city fell, Alexander had instructed the troops to take no prisoners. The sack, and the violence that accompanied it, had the immediate impact of the neighbouring city of Andaca surrendering immediately without incident, the inhabitants being spared the horror experienced by their neighbours.

From Andaca, Alexander marched east into the Kunar Valley. By this time his reputation for savagery and brutality was preceding him; in every town he encountered in that valley the inhabitants fled into the mountains before he arrived. The abandoned towns and cities that he encountered were occupied and then almost completely destroyed, causing thousands of people to become refugees. Alexander's army also had constant need for supplies, resulting in these natives being made homeless and with neither the means of supporting themselves nor stores of crops that remained un-looted.

As a furtherance of his policy of militarizing the region that he began before crossing the Hindu Kush, Alexander founded another city in a strategically important location; this is a direct copy of the policy conducted in Sogdiana that had both caused the revolt, and helped to suppress it.[209] The fact that this policy had already begun in Sogdiana, with the result that the region became increasingly volatile and unstable, meant that it had to be extended to keep the region under any semblance of control. Alexander had started along a path that he could not stop until the region was properly suppressed.

Massaga

After almost two years of continuous mountain campaigning against enemies conducting guerrilla warfare in Bactria and Sogdiana, Alexander had become adept in dealing with these tactics. From the Kunar Valley, he marched into the Bajaur region where he left Coenus with a detachment to besiege the city of Beira. The Aspasians in this region offered little more than an inconvenience to the Macedonians, and they did not delay there for long. The Assacenians of Swat were a different matter, however.

The king of the Assaceni in the Lower Swat valley, named Assacanus (although Curtius tells us that he had died shortly before Alexander's arrival and they were now ruled by his mother, Cleophis), commanded a substantial force of some 30,000 infantry and 2,000 cavalry, which was further strengthened by a significant group of Indian mercenaries, perhaps 7,000 strong.[210] Alexander's reputation as a commander of unparalleled ability was also preceding him, as Assacanus evidently realized that, despite having an army that was roughly equivalent to Alexander's (although much larger than the advanced force Alexander was currently commanding), they were not of the quality to defeat the Macedonians in open battle. Assacanus, therefore, decided that his best chance of victory was to retire to a number of local strongholds, the most important of which was Massaga, located in the region of the Katgala Pass.

Massaga was yet another formidable natural defensive position, bordered by a fast flowing river with sheer banks to the west preventing any approach, and by steep cliffs to the south. Curtius describes the fortress location as:[211]

> A barricade of beetling crags, at the foot of which lie caves and chasms hollowed to a great depth over a long period of time. Where these terminate, a ditch of massive proportions forms a barrier.

These mud brick walls were further reinforced by a wooden superstructure. The city itself was protected by massive walls over 7km long, their lower sections made of stone, the upper of unbaked brick bound together by pebbles. Alexander arrived outside of the city with a relatively small force and perhaps felt it too small to directly and successfully assault the city. Either way, he drew up in position on the flat ground some distance from the fortress. Arrian tells us that the intention was to draw the enemy out onto ground of Alexander's choosing and therefore avoid the necessity of a time-consuming and costly siege:[212]

> It was clear to Alexander that the fight would take place close to the town; he determined, therefore, to draw the enemy on, in order to ensure that, if they were repulsed – as he was certain they would be – they would not have a short and easy way of retreat within the protection of their walls.

This tactic is one that is frequently repeated during Alexander's career, both in sieges and especially set-piece battles, that of luring the enemy onto ground of his choosing, and can be considered to be another one of Alexander's hallmark tactics. The tactic, in this instance, was a little more complex than usual. Alexander apparently set up his troops on the flat ground mentioned above at a distance of perhaps 0.5-1km from the city. The tactic worked admirably, and the Indians were lured onto the plain. They initially had not realized the relative lack of size of the Macedonian force when they had refused the set-piece battle by withdrawing to their fortress, an error they were attempting to rectify before any other Macedonian troops made an appearance. Arrian also implies that finances were short for Assacanus, and the need to pay the 7,000 Indian mercenaries for the duration of their service would have been expensive. These financial considerations were a potentially significant factor in the decision to sally forth from the safety of the walls.

The Indians began to emerge from the city and started to set up on the plain before its gates. Once Alexander was sure they were indeed sallying out in force, he ordered his troops to withdraw:[213]

> To a piece of high ground rather less than a mile from the position he had originally intended to take up. This apparent sign of defeat put fresh fire into the enemy.

As noted by Arrian, the withdrawal was entirely misunderstood by the less disciplined Indians; they took it as a sign of defeat, that the Macedonians were fleeing before them. The Indians, apparently before properly forming up, charged towards the Macedonians in their new more defensive position on high ground. The distance they would have had to cross, perhaps 2km, most of the way in a disordered run, would have left them both tired and utterly disorganized when they finally reached the Macedonian ranks. This is highly reminiscent of the tactic used by both Miltiades at Marathon and Philip at Chaeronaea of feigning retreat only to turn around, reform and strike a disorganized enemy when they were most vulnerable.

Macedonian discipline again proved the decisive factor; when the Indians were within missile range, Alexander ordered the troops to stop and about face and ordered the archers to engage the enemy whist forming up the heavy infantry who immediately began to march in close order down the hill towards the enemy. This siege is one of the few instances where we see Alexander positioned with the heavy infantry, rather than with a cavalry unit. The Indians apparently could not stop their headlong charge in time and they ran straight into the ordered ranks of the Macedonian heavy infantry. The result was all too predictable: there was a brief and bloody struggle during which the Indians turned and fled back to their city, probably with even greater alacrity than that shown in advancing upon the Macedonians in the first instance. The only recorded losses were 200 Indians, not many at all when we consider the size of their force at 39,000. The psychological impact was of far greater importance than the actual loss of manpower, however. They had seen first hand the discipline and fighting quality of the Macedonians, and they would have been concerned to say the least.

Alexander continued to march his troops, maintaining their close order, until he was as close to the walls as he could get. Alexander now faced a difficult and challenging siege, and was initially at a loss for what to do as the caverns at the foot of the walls prevented a direct assault:[214]

> Alexander surveyed the fortifications, uncertain how to proceed; for the caverns could be filled only with earth, and only by filling them could siege engines be brought up to the walls.

While investigating the defences, Alexander strayed too close and was hit in the leg or ankle by an arrow shot from the walls. Curtius tells us that he tore the barb from the wound and, without even bandaging the wound, completed his reconnaissance of the walls. Arrian has no delay at all between Alexander's survey of the defences, the wound to his leg and the commencement of the siege, but there was simply no way that Alexander could have begun the siege that quickly. Arrian has siege towers and catapults appear from nowhere and begin the bombardment immediately. Curtius has a nine-day delay as Alexander demolished the buildings that had spilled out of the city as its population grew. The rubble that came from these buildings, coupled with a number of massive tree trunks, was thrown into the caverns that were effectively acting as a moat around the fortress.[215] This delay in filling in the moat was an essential for Alexander; his baggage train would have been some distance behind this small advance column, and without it he would have been reduced to using scaling ladders that could be easily manufactured on site. The siege train arrived with consummate timing, however. Just as the caverns had been filled to a point that the ground was effectively level, Alexander brought up his towers and catapults and began the siege proper.

The defenders were not experienced in modern siege techniques, or in modern technology, as Curtius tells us:[216]

> Particularly terrifying for the people with no experience of such contrivances were the moveable towers and, since the huge structures relied on no observable means of propulsion, the townspeople believed they were driven by divine power. They also claimed that the

Macedonians wall-fighting pikes and the heavy spears hurled from the engines were not weapons such as mortals used.

The fortifications, however formidable, were not up to the standards of fourth century siege warfare, which had been redefined by Alexander and his stone-throwing catapults. A breach was quickly forced in the defensive circuit, and the Macedonians immediately attempted to make a breakthrough. The defenders offered stout resistance, however, and the hypaspists who formed the assault group were driven back. On the second day after the breach was made, Alexander brought forward a siege tower and packed it with missile troops who laid down a suppressing fire against the defenders in an attempt to keep them from the walls and the breach to allow the hypaspists time to gain entry. Again the Macedonians were driven back by the now-increasingly-desperate defenders. On the third day the towers were again brought forward and a bridge thrown over the breach. 'Over this he led his Guards, the unit which, by the same tactic, had helped him to the capture of Tyre.'[217] At this point even Arrian recognizes Alexander using the same tactics, even using the same units to achieve them, as he had done in previous sieges (Alexander was ever the great recycler of successful tactics). The construction of the tower's bridge was flawed, however, and coupled with the hypaspists being too keen to get across, the bridge collapsed. Those who survived the fall found themselves the subject of a rain of arrows and other missiles from the defenders on the walls, whilst others sortied from the walls to slaughter those who were wounded and could not escape. Alexander ordered forward some troops to recover the injured as soon as he could, but many lives were lost before the rescue column arrived.

The following day the same tactic was repeated with another tower and another bridge, this time with far greater success. The Indian mercenary troops that were fighting in the front lines acquitted themselves admirably whilst their commander lived. But when he was killed by a missile shot from a catapult, their bravery disintegrated. At the death of their commander, the Indian mercenaries sued for peace and were allowed to join Alexander's army. It would appear, however, that the desertion was nothing more than a ruse by the Indians. We are told that they intended to join Alexander in the short term to survive the immediate danger of the siege, but then to slip away quietly during the night, not wishing to take up arms against their fellow Indians. Before they could enact their plan, however, Alexander had their camp surrounded the following night and gave the order that they were to be massacred to a man before they had any chance of enacting their plan. Diodorus attributes gross treachery to Alexander, claiming that they were attacked and slaughtered without justification. This was undoubtedly one of Alexander's worst atrocities.[218]

Probably after the defection of the Indians, the defenders abandoned the outer walls and retired to the citadel, but their position was now desperate and they had no option but to offer their surrender. It is interesting to note that there is no mention of the thousands of other native troops noted earlier in the narratives of the siege. They sent a deputation of leading citizens to Alexander to ask for terms, and Alexander, rather surprisingly given recent events, accepted. Curtius tells us:[219]

> The queen came with a group of ladies of noble birth who made libations from golden bowls. The queen herself placed her little son at Alexander's knees, and from him gained not only a pardon but also the restitution of her former status, for she retained the title of queen.

He goes on to imply that Alexander was enamoured of the queen's beauty, and that this was why the city was spared the horror that the Macedonians had visited upon so many others in recent years. He also notes that the queen subsequently bore a son she named Alexander 'whoever his father was'.

Massaga was not, in reality, a huge city and certainly not as difficult to assault as Tyre or the Sogdian Rock had been – but it was certainly no push over. Alexander demonstrated both his tactical awareness and a realization of the weakness of his position (that he possessed no siege engines, for example). By not immediately assaulting the city he showed that he was not blinded by the myth of his own invincibility. Luring the defenders onto flat ground outside of the city was a clever ruse and could easily have worked, but he was not able to reach the city before the fleeing attackers had all reached safety; if his heavy infantry had been less disciplined and broken their close order to give a headlong chase, as they followed the routing Indians, he may well have done. He also demonstrated during this siege that, yet again, natural barriers were simply obstacles that were there to be overcome. The treatment of the defenders after their submission is interesting; he was probably trying to demonstrate that those who willingly surrendered to his rule received generous treatment, especially after the excesses of the recent campaign.

Ora and Bazira

After the fall of Massaga, the army was again divided into a number of flying columns, which had by now become standard practice during the campaign on the northeast frontier. This policy had the effect of allowing Alexander to conquer more territory, to do so with greater speed as smaller columns moved rather more quickly, and to reduce the logistical difficulties of having the whole army together for a march in difficult and unknown terrain. With this further division of the army, Coenus was sent to blockade the city of Bazira whilst Attalus, Alcetas and Demetrius advanced upon Ora, probably to be associated with the modern Ude-Gram as identified by Stein.[220] Attalus was instructed to blockade the town pending Alexander's arrival, and presumably to make preparations for a siege, if preparations were required (such as the bridging of a chasm for example, or the construction of siege engines). This is a curious instruction and suggests either Attalus' force was very small and not capable of carrying the siege, or that Alexander wanted the glory of the capture himself, or perhaps that Alexander was growing impatient of the preparations that were required before each siege and he was trying to save himself time by ensuring that as soon as he arrived before the city, he could launch his assault. Whatever the reason for the orders, the defenders were not prepared to sit and wait for the arrival of greater numbers of Macedonian troops, and made a sally against Alcestas' force soon after it arrived; they were quickly repulsed, however. At this point Alexander was undecided as to whether to make for Bazira or Ora first. The decision was effectively made for him by the news that Bazira was in a better defensive position, and that the townspeople showed no signs of surrender. Alexander initially set off for Bazira but quickly diverted his men to Ora upon receiving a report that some of the Indians in the region were gathering under the leadership of Abisares with the intention of moving secretly to Ora to help defend the city. Alexander made straight for Ora:[221]

> Sending an order to Coenus to construct a blockhouse outside Bazira, garrison it sufficiently to prevent the people of the town from making free use of the surrounding country, and then join him with the remainder of his troops.

Again we have the strong implication that there were very few troops operating with Alexander in this region. The remainder must have been campaigning elsewhere, or following on slowly behind. Most likely Alexander's flying column was conquering areas and the remainder of the army moving more slowly whilst conducting final mopping up operations once Alexander had moved on. The fact that Alexander needed the bulk of Coenus' detachment tells us that he was undermanned and that he took the threat posed by Abisares' Indians seriously. Alexander would also have been conscious of his experience outside Pellium, where he was engaging a city and found himself trapped by newly-arrived reinforcements.

The Indians in Bazira watched Coenus withdraw with the bulk of the Macedonians with joy. They assumed, with natural contempt for the invaders, that they were withdrawing in fear and that the remainder would be easy prey for an Indian sortie. Probably within a day of Coenus moving off, the Indians made a sally from Bazira. The engagement was rapid and bloody; at its conclusion, 500 Indians lay dead on the field and more than 70 were captured. After this, the defenders were so shaken that they did not make another move against the remaining Macedonians, whilst the Macedonians strengthened their own fortifications outside of the town and awaited the return of Coenus or Alexander to complete the reduction of the city.

The siege of Ora gave Alexander no problems at all. The city fell at the first assault and the expected relief column led by Abisares never materialized. It is also evident that the town was not as well defended, either in troops or by nature, as some of the fortresses that Alexander had encountered in the previous two years. With the fall of Ora, Alexander also captured a number of elephants that had been left there. This is the second reference to elephants in the sources, the first being at Gaugamela where they almost certainly were not present (taking no part in any of the battle narratives at all). It could be, therefore, that this was the first time the Macedonians had encountered elephants, and not when they faced Porus at the Hydaspes in 327.

When news arrived in Bazira of the fate of those defending Ora, they realized that their position was hopeless, especially given their abject failure in the sortie against Alexander's blockading force; if they could not even defeat Coenus then what hope would they have once Alexander returned? At midnight of the day following the fall of Ora, the Indians inhabiting Bazira abandoned the town and melted away into the surrounding countryside, as had happened so often in the previous few months. They were not simply abandoning the city, however. Resistance was still their intention: they gathered together with what would today be called local insurgents, and made their way to the imposing fortifications of the Aornus Rock.

The Rock of Aornus

After Alexander had occupied a virtually-empty city and garrisoned it (as well as Ora in order to provide a permanent military presence in this unsettled region), he set off in the direction of the Indus River and the Rock of Aornus. Along his route a number of minor towns surrendered without resistance to Alexander, and were also occupied. These towns surrendered to the Macedonians partly out of fear of Alexander's reputation, and partly because Alexander had with him a number of 'local chiefs' from the region; namely Cophaeus and Assagetes. The use of the local nobility was a major strategic variation from his early campaigns and demonstrates once again Alexander's desire to bring those he conquered on-board with the expedition and into the growing empire. This policy is also seen in the recruiting of the 30,000 youths and the increasing use of Oriental troops in the cavalry units.

After a march of probably only a few days, Alexander arrived at Embolima (which Curtius calls Ecbolima), a town close to Aornus, and a perfect base of operations against the fortress.[222] Sir Aurel Stein was the first to identify the Rock of Aornus with the modern Pir-Sar in 1926, although he didn't produce his book until three years later. Stein described the mountain as follows:[223]

> Pir-sar is but one of a series of narrow spurs which… range, stretching east from above Upal, throws out to the south before it drops rapidly and flattens out fanlike towards the low plateau of Maira, washed at its foot by the Indus. Of those spurs Pir-Sar preserves its height for the longest distance, and owing to the uniform level and the very fertile soil of its summit, affords most scope both for cultivation and grazing. The practically level portion of the top extends at an average elevation of about 7,100 feet for over a mile and a half. At its upper end this flat portion is bordered for some distance by gentle slopes equally suited for such use… Pir-Sar forms a dominating position over-looking all the other spurs.

Stein described the site after travelling around the region extensively; his identification has been questioned, but not conclusively disproved as yet. It has the advantage of tallying closely with Arrian's account, which gives a height of 8,000ft and describes the Rock in similar terms to Stein, also noting the abundant natural water springs on the plateau. This final point is key, as it meant they were better equipped than some more naturally-strong defensive positions, as all they needed to store was food, not water. What Stein does not say is that the summit is of a very significant size, having a circumference of some 40km.

This natural fortress was known to the Greeks. Legend, as reported by Curtius, tells us that Heracles himself had attempted to storm the city and failed.

Diodorus has a slightly less violent account, but Heracles fails in his attempt none the less:[224]

> It is said that Heracles of old thought to lay siege to this 'rock' but refrained because of the occurrence of certain sharp earthquake shocks and other divine signs, and this made Alexander even more eager to capture the stronghold when he heard it, and so to rival the god's reputation.

Even if it were not for the opportunity to outdo Heracles, Alexander would still have besieged the fortress. It was an opportunity to test his skills yet again and Alexander simply could not have passed without making the attempt. He could also not allow large numbers of un-subdued Indians to remain free on his lines of supply and communication, with the inherent dangers that presented.

The local tribal chiefs, Cophaeus and Assagates, would have told Alexander of the impregnable nature of Aornus, and immediately upon arrival at Embolima, Craterus was detached from the army with orders to gather supplies from the surrounding countryside, as well as its towns and villages. Enough supplies were to be gathered together to survive the protracted siege that Alexander expected. Although Alexander was no doubt expecting a lengthy siege, he still would have wanted to carry the fortress by assault if at all possible. In an attempt to do so he set off immediately with:[225]

> The archers, the Agrianians, Coenus' *taxis*, the best-armed and most active of the other infantry units, 200 Companions and 100 mounted archers.

It is unclear why Alexander took 300 cavalry with his assault party. Perhaps to provide a means of mobile protection in the event of an ambush en-route, or perhaps more likely these troops were here being used as infantry. Horse archers were likely of a higher quality with greater accuracy than regular infantry archers. This was a relatively large force for an initial probing assault, or at the very least a reconnaissance mission. They would have quickly discovered that they were ill prepared or equipped to undertake a direct assault against this formidable fortress.

We must examine Alexander's strategic decision to besiege Aornus at all. Alexander could easily have blockaded the fortress with a relatively small force (much the size of the initial assault/reconnaissance force) and moved the main army on towards India to carry on with the campaign. The defenders would have been penned in with no easy means of exit from the fortress; its natural defences would have worked in reverse too, acting as a prison, and they would have had no opportunity to spread disaffection amongst the local population. The siege of Aornus is a fine example of Alexander's character impinging on strategic decisions; it was simply not in his nature to allow a fortress to stand against him effectively unchallenged. This was a very different situation from Tyre, as that city had to be captured in order to affect the strategic defeat of the Persian navy, or Halicarnassus where he did leave the city before it was conquered and left a small force to complete the reduction. At Halicarnassus, however, he had completed much of that siege himself before moving on.

Alexander's advanced force marched towards Aornus slowly. In reality it was more for reconnaissance than in any real belief that this force would capture the fortress, and events bear this out. Over the course of a day or two it made a number of small and slow advances, stopping each time at a convenient and safe point. This indicates two things. Firstly, that Alexander was cautious of being ambushed by the defenders; Indians in a number of cities had shown themselves willing to sally from their defences if they saw the opportunity to inflict heavy losses on the attacker. Secondly, Alexander was investigating the terrain and topography of the area thoroughly, looking for a potential means of attack, however unorthodox, including back routes to the summit and so on.

During one of these pauses, Alexander was approached by a number of natives who, in return for his protection, would guide him to the most vulnerable point of the fortress. This proved to be a ridge that overlooked the Rock fortress, a ridge now called Bar-Sar. Alexander, of course, immediately accepted the offer and ordered Ptolemy with a hand picked force consisting of the Agrianians, a detachment of hypaspists and 'the other light armed units', probably the archers, to occupy the ridge, fortify it and inform the king by signal when this was complete. In order that the defenders remained unaware that Alexander had discovered this higher ridge, Ptolemy was ordered to march at night and without the benefit of torches; we can only imagine how dangerous this kind of operation was on these rocky slopes.

Whatever the dangers, Ptolemy was successful in first gaining, and then securing the heights with a ditch and stockade, and early the following morning sent a fire signal to Alexander that he was in position. Alexander was already prepared to make a frontal assault, and as soon as he saw Ptolemy's signal, he ordered the advance. Alexander's frontal assault was fought at close quarters and the Indians must, therefore, have left the relative safety of Pir-Sar and occupied what is now called the Danda-Nurdai spur, adjacent to Pir-Sar.[226] The skirmish was brief and bloody; Alexander encountered tremendous difficulty from the terrain and the Indians fought stoutly, driving back the attackers. In Arrian's words, Alexander's assault 'achieved nothing'. As soon as Alexander's assault was stopped, the Indians turned their attention to Ptolemy's force that was occupying the ridge. They realized the strategic importance of this area, and it should be considered a significant tactical error that they had not secured it before Alexander's arrival. The Indian assault on the stockade is vividly described by Arrian:[227]

> They moved to the attack, and there was a fierce struggle, the Indians doing all they could to tear down the stockade, while Ptolemy fought to maintain his hold. The weight of the Macedonian missiles overpowered the Indians, who at nightfall were forced to withdraw.

It was clear to Alexander that another frontal assault would have the same effect, and he could not afford a siege of attrition. Arrian does not make it clear why the assault failed so badly, simply noting the difficulties in the terrain. Diodorus and Curtius both mention a ravine at the foot of the rock, now called the Burimar Ravine, which goes a long way to explaining the difficulty.[228]

The night after the failed frontal assault, Alexander selected one of several Indian deserters, or more likely one of his local guides who had special knowledge of the area, to carry a message to Ptolemy. Ptolemy was ordered not simply to be happy to maintain his defensive position, but to assault the enemy at a pre-arranged signal. The intention was to link the two forces and offer the Indians a coordinated two pronged assault, an identical tactic of attacking the enemy in more than one direction that we see repeatedly through Alexander's career.

At dawn of the following day, Alexander, with a picked detachment of troops, began to march along the same track that Ptolemy had used a week earlier to reach Bar-Sar. By attempting to link up his two forces he believed that the assault would be carried far more effectively. It would also allow him to further reinforce the heights with fresh troops. The morning's fighting was again difficult and many more died on both sides. The Indians used the natural defence of being higher than the attackers to launch missiles of all kinds (arrows, rocks etc.) against the attackers in a desperate attempt to drive them off. By noon, after a morning of hard fighting, Alexander made contact with Ptolemy; the now reunited force together began an assault on the fortress. The assault was again a failure and was abandoned, probably along with Bar-Sar.

In order for Alexander to make a successful frontal assault again, the ravine needed to be bridged to allow catapults to be brought to bear against the defenders. This was a tried and tested tactic of Alexander that he had used repeatedly at earlier sieges: if a natural obstacle stood in the way, remove it. We see many examples of this, first at Tyre, and then on several occasions in Bactria, Sogdiana and now in India. The sources all speak in terms of the ravine being filled rather than bridged, but the shear volume of space that would have to be filled surely precludes this possibility. A bridge spanning the gap would be a major engineering feat, but more practical than filling the ravine.

Alexander ordered the trees in a nearby forest to be stripped, felled and hauled to the ravine with a view to constructing a bridge across the 450m chasm, and avoiding the 180m drop, Alexander as always leading the way by felling the first tree. Curtius tells us that the bridge was constructed within seven days of Alexander felling that first tree; this seems a remarkable rate of construction, although Arrian seems to be faster still:[229]

> During the first day the earthwork was carried forward about 180m; by the second, slingers and catapults operating from the portion already completed were able to check enemy raids on the men still working; within three days the entire space was filled.

In reality what Arrian is telling us is that after four days, the work was advanced enough for the defenders to be engaged, but that work continued after that point. Thus Curtius' seven days (or perhaps more) is feasible.

In an echo of the successful tactic at the Sogdian Rock, Alexander ordered the archers, Agrianians and thirty of the bravest young men to scale the cliffs in order to regain the heights above Pir-Sar. This time the attempt was made during the day, and the Indians were expecting it and had prepared their missile troops to pepper the mountaineers. Missiles of all kinds rained down upon them, and many slipped from the cliffs into the fast-flowing waters below. Slowly, after a long and arduous climb with the ever present danger of slipping to their death, or being struck by missiles launched by the defenders, more and more troops gained the heights and began to engage the Indians in hand-to-hand combat. Alexander's use of archers on this mission was important as they could return fire as the Agrianians fought their way to Bar-Sar. Gradually the Indians were forced from the heights and the Agrianians secured their objective, which was again now fortified with a stockade, as Ptolemy had done earlier.

The Indians now realized the difficulty of their position. They had once again lost the high ground with the tactical advantage that it afforded the Macedonians, as well as the fact that the bridge was close enough that Alexander could bring his artillery to bear. From this point it was only a matter of time for the defenders. The Indian resolve crumbled and they sent envoys to Alexander to sue for peace. Arrian tells us that they expected to be able to draw out the discussions until night fall when they intended to abandon their position and melt away into the surrounding mountains. Alexander was now used to this Indian tactic of abandoning a hopeless position, and he expected them to do just that. He therefore stationed a number of hypaspists along the only escape routes off the plateau, and, at a pre-arranged signal, ordered them to fall upon the escaping Indians that very night. Alexander was now left in possession of a fortress that even Heracles had failed to conquer.

The rapidity of the construction of the bridge is yet another testimony, if one were needed, to the quality of Alexander's engineers. They were constantly called upon to make the impossible a reality, and in remarkably short periods of time. The bridges that were constructed in Sogdiana, and here at Aornus, only took a few days; modern engineers would find it difficult if not impossible to match these feats, even though they were temporary structures.

At Aornus Alexander put the lives of his irreplaceable men at risk on a whim. He could easily have isolated the Rock at little cost in manpower and moved on, but ego, or perhaps pride, would not allow this. The local story of Heracles' failure to capture the Rock was all the incentive he would have needed, much like with the Gordian Knot in Asia Minor, or the later crossing of the Gedrosian Desert in emulation of Queen Sisigambis, Alexander simply did not possess the will to resist a seemingly impossible challenge.

After the fall of Aornus, Alexander marched to Embolima where he received a report that the brother of Oxyartes, Erices, had blockaded a narrow pass on the road towards India with a force of some 20,000 men and 15 elephants.[230] Curtius tells us, advancing quickly with apparently only the slingers and archers, he dislodged the defenders from the pass and scattered them. This is an example of Curtius' exaggeration, or simply a mistake. Alexander commanded no more than 2,000 archers and slingers, and it seems unlikely, to say the least, that these missile troops, with no back up of heavy infantry or cavalry, could have carried a pass commanded by a force ten times its size.

After crossing the Indus River, Alexander entered Taxila. Almost immediately he was met by King Taxiles who brought Alexander some much needed supplies. Alexander's next stop was the Hydaspes River and a set-piece cavalry battle with Porus that is described in the forthcoming volume *The Field Campaigns of Alexander the Great*.

Following victory at the Hydaspes River, Alexander resumed his march east towards the Indian Ocean, after first leaving Craterus evidently to construct a further series of outposts in Porus' realm.[231] These were military stations intended to keep order in this newly-conquered territory. Alexander had no idea if the territory would remain loyal after he left, and posts such as these were set up all across the east of this new empire.

Arrian tells us of a series of campaigns against some thirty-seven cities in the area between the Hydaspes and Acesines, east of Porus' kingdom, although he gives us no detail of them and we can learn nothing of Alexander's siege techniques as a result. Of these thirty-seven cities, the smallest apparently contained around 5,000 people, the largest more than double this. That the numbers are exaggerated hardly seems worth mentioning, but the fact is that the campaigning continued apace. Along with a number of minor campaigns, the only one deserving of mention is the siege of Sangala.

Sangala

Alexander's intelligence network had informed him that an independent Indian tribe called the Cathaei were, along with some others, preparing to resist. Alexander immediately set off in their direction and, after a two day march, found himself in the vicinity of the city of Sangala, at the town of Pimprama, which was ruled by the Adraistae. The city of Sangala had a reputation for being strongly fortified, and the Cathaei of being formidable warriors. Alexander by now considered India to be his territory, even the areas where he had not yet been, and any resistance was an affront to his rule and must, therefore, be crushed. They were also supported in their defiance of Alexander by two other tribes, the Oxydracae and the Malli.

The Adraistae offered Alexander no resistance and the following day he rested his men before setting off for Sangala. The Cathaei and their allies had taken up a position on a hill in front of the city and awaited Alexander's approach. The hill was steep and some of the sides were difficult for an attacking force to easily climb. To further strengthen their position the defenders had set up a temporary palisade of carts which formed a triple ring around the central mound of the hill. This was in effect three separate walls so that if the attackers got past the first, a second and third manned wall awaited them. Their intention was to break the Macedonian infantry's formation as they passed through or over the outer carts, thus allowing the defenders to fall upon a disorganized enemy. Alexander did what he always did: in the words of Arrian, 'Alexander modified his tactics to suit the circumstances'.[232]

Instead of blindly attacking the defenders with an immediate frontal assault, Alexander used the same tactic that had been so successful only weeks earlier at the Hydaspes: he opened the battle with his Dahae horse archers firing upon the defenders from a distance. This time it was to prevent the defenders attacking Alexander's forces whilst they were still deploying. Arrian again, as at the Hydaspes, mentions Cleitus as a cavalry commander. His hipparchy had evidently performed well enough at the Hydaspes for him to be promoted to its permanent command. Arrian also mentions the 'special cavalry hipparchy' in conjunction with Cleitus' cavalry command. This special hipparchy, I would argue, was that which Cleitus had commanded at the Hydaspes. If this is the case then it was the cavalry that were recruited in Bactria and Sogdiana that he had commanded briefly in that region after they had joined Alexander. Cleitus was evidently transferred from this hipparchy to another one, presumably one whose hipparch had been killed at the Hydaspes. The fact that the Persian cavalry were still closely linked to Cleitus is in recognition of his special bond with those troops, having commanded them in the Bactria/Sogdiana region, as well as at the Hydaspes. This special cavalry hipparchy can not have been the *agema*, as Arrian uses that term specifically of that unit; they were something different from the normal troops and can only have been the Persians formerly commanded by Cleitus.

After the Dahae had covered the advance of the army successfully, Cleitus' new hipparchy was ordered to the right wing, as described by Arrian:[233]

> he brought Cleitus' mounted regiment and the special cavalry round to the right wing of his army, with the guards and Agrianians in close touch… before his dispositions were complete, the rear-guard, both horse and foot, arrived on the scene; the cavalry was used to strengthen the wings, and the additional infantry units to increase the solidity of the phalanx.

Alexander also seemingly employed a second line, as in his set-piece battles, although he would not have expected to have need for such a device. The only major difference between Sangala and the earlier set-piece battles was the strength of that rear guard. This guard was not a tactical requirement of the battle as there was almost no possibility of the enemy breaking through the Macedonian lines, but a large reserve was employed simply because the front line would have been very short, and there was not enough space to locate all of the front line troops in their usual positions. The one thing that this does tell us is that Alexander's army at Sangala was of a more significant size than during some of the earlier sieges. This was not simply some flying column, although his inability to completely surround the town during the second phase of the siege tells us that the entire army was not present. We have no information as to where the secondary columns were campaigning, but that is not so unusual. The sources are almost always Alexander-centric in their approach, understandably.

The Macedonian order of battle before Sangala, therefore, shows a very traditional pattern; heavy infantry in the centre, the hypaspists and Agrianians to their right and cavalry (as well as detachments of archers) on both wings, almost exactly the same as the set up in almost every military encounter in Alexander's career.

Alexander moved to the right of the army, again as was tradition, and took command of the cavalry in that sector. He had noticed that the defensive palisade of wagons was slightly more widely dispersed opposite the cavalry of the right, and the hill less steep there than in other areas, so a cavalry attack was possible. After seeing this potential weakness (although it could, of course, have been a trap to entice the Macedonian cavalry to attack a fortified position at a significant disadvantage), Alexander began the advance with the cavalry. Alexander did not make straight for the gaps in the defensive line, but used his horse archers to move along the line in an attempt to lure out the defenders, a tactic that was so common during his career, and usually worked. On this occasion, however, they did not bite. The defenders clambered onto their carts and met the Dahae arrows with arrows of their own, but did not venture beyond the protection of their improvised palisade.

Alexander's opening gambit had failed, but it was not a decisive failure as it had cost him little in terms of manpower. Another tactic, however, was evidently required to break through the defences. This failure did not delay Alexander for long, as soon as the cavalry units reached the safety of their original position in the line (so as to avoid confusion of deploying infantry through the still-moving cavalry units), Alexander's superiority in numbers allowed him to surround the wagons with his heavy infantry in order to attack the carts from all sides.[234] Once the infantry were in position, the king dismounted, joined them and immediately began another assault. Curtius tells us that the unorthodox defensive tactics of the Cathaeans caused some disarray among the Macedonians, but he overplays the situation somewhat.[235] When the assault began, the outer defences were no match for the Macedonian heavy infantry, and the Cathaei were quickly driven back to their second line of carts. As was their plan, the defenders immediately rallied upon gaining the second layer of defence and set themselves up to oppose Alexander's continued advance. Their discipline in reforming upon gaining the safety of the second ring of carts speaks volumes as to their training, and of their tactical plan of defence in depth.

The effect of a ring of carts was that, every time the defenders were driven back, their defence became more stout as they were defending a smaller circuit; it also meant that the defenders became increasingly fierce in their resistance as they could see only one more layer to fall back upon before they had nowhere to retreat to. With the fall of the first ring, the defenders were now in a closer order and the Macedonians had lost the advantage of moving in unbroken formations across open ground (albeit hilly open ground). In order to regain some of the initiative, Alexander had the outer ring of carts removed to the base of the hill so that the Macedonians could advance upon the second ring without having to cross a barrier first.

As the Macedonians pressed the inner rings, the fighting became more brutal and casualties would have been higher on both sides than during the attack on the outer ring. Despite this, the defenders were also quickly driven back from the second ring, but they did not withdraw to their 'keep', the final inner ring of carts. The Cathaeans in fact withdrew to the relative safety of the town, after suffering significant losses. Alexander rested his troops the remainder of the day. Falling back to the city was entirely sensible on the part of the Cathaei. They had failed to hold the carts against the Macedonians and throwing away their lives would be futile; much better to live to fight another day behind the greater (and permanent) defences of the city. Despite this, the defenders had lost up to 8,000 men in their defence of the hill, although this figure cited by Curtius probably refers to the total losses for the campaign, rather than this opening sequence.[236]

The following morning Alexander ordered the city to be surrounded as best he could, although he did not possess enough troops to allow a complete encirclement. The only gap in the infantry line was opposite a lake close to the city. The waters of the lake were shallow enough to be able to cross, and Alexander anticipated that the Indians might try and escape as they had done in earlier sieges when their situation became hopeless. To prevent this, on the far side of this lake, Alexander stationed his cavalry who were instructed to patrol the area, thus effectively sealing the only gap in the line. Alexander's guess proved correct and under cover of night (Alexander apparently spent the entire day setting up his circumvallation) the defenders slipped out of the city to attempt to cross the lake. Many of the Indians were caught completely by surprise by Alexander's cavalry patrols and were slaughtered as they tried to escape. The Indians quickly realized what was happening and those who survived recovered their wits rapidly enough to make it back to the transient security of the town.

After setting up his positions the previous day, and successfully luring the Indians into his carefully-laid trap, he ordered the construction of his own double stockade around the city, and increased the patrols around the lake to ensure no Indian managed to escape alive. Alexander had delayed the onset of the siege to allow his siege train to arrive; at that point the bombardment could begin and the city be taken. It still had not arrived, however, and there was no information as to when it was due. Alexander also learned from an Indian deserter (we can only assume there must have been a steady stream of them at this point), that the remaining defenders were planning to make another attempt to cross the lake and escape the following night. Upon hearing this news of the impending second breakout attempt, Alexander ordered Ptolemy to take up a position close to the lake with the hypaspists, archers and Agrianians to prevent any Indians escaping. Alexander went on to say, according to Arrian:[237]

> The instant, he [Alexander] said to Ptolemy, you see them at it, stop them, and order the trumpeter to sound the alarm. On this signal, the rest of you officers will take your men promptly to the scene of the action, wherever the trumpet calls you. And, mark you, I shall be there myself.

Similar orders would have been given to all of the officers as it is implied that Alexander was anticipating a breakout somewhere, and he was preparing for the possibility that the Indian deserters were wrong in claiming it would be across the water, as previously.

To prepare his position, Ptolemy gathered some of the carts that the Cathaei had used in the defence of the hill several days before, and stationed them at random intervals along the route that he anticipated the Indians would take as they slipped out of the city. The intention was that these would act as obstacles in the darkness (evidently it was cloudy, and therefore very dark) and would cause confusion amongst those attempting to escape. This also tells us that the route to the lake must have been hidden from the city by some obstacle, perhaps a copse of trees, or the defenders would have known the carts were there, and the potential confusion would have been partially obviated. Ptolemy also ordered that the stockade be extended around the full circumference of the city closing the gap that had existed between the city and the lake. This construction work was completed quickly and entirely under cover of darkness.

Alexander's Indian deserters proved correct: some time in the early hours of the morning, at the fourth watch by Roman reckoning, the gates that faced the lake were opened and the defenders began to slip out. Ptolemy and the hypaspists were in perfect position, however. Once they were out of the city, and could not easily slip back in as with the first attempted breakout, Ptolemy ordered the trumpets to be sounded, and they began to advance upon the Cathaei. The Indians' expected escape route was already blocked by carts and the hastily-constructed stockade. The presence of these unexpected obstacles coupled with the hypaspists falling upon them, resulted in tremendous confusion and panic within the Indian ranks. The Macedonians showed no mercy. Arrian noted that they were 'cutting down every man who managed to struggle through between the carts'. We can only assume, although this is never explicitly stated, that women and children would also be amongst those trying to escape their expected fate once the town fell. These would likely have received much the same treatment as distinguishing between them at night would have been very difficult. The Indians, realizing that they had failed again in their attempts to escape managed to get back to the city, at a loss of some 500 of their number.[238]

At around the time of the second attempted break out, or perhaps shortly afterwards, Porus arrived with his remaining army of 'the rest of his elephants and 5,000 Indian troops'.[238] Given that we know that Alexander captured all of the elephants left alive after the Hydaspes, Porus must not have committed his entire reserve to that battle. The arrival of these reserves coincided with Alexander's engineers having completed the construction of the siege engines that they had been working upon, as well as perhaps the arrival of some siege equipment with Porus. These siege engines were brought up into a position where they could begin the bombardment of the walls. During what must have been a couple of weeks between Alexander's arrival, and the arrival of Porus, Alexander's engineers were busy. They had been working on building siege engines, and completing the double stockade. They had also evidently been conducting sapping operations beneath the city walls. We can assume this only because as soon as Alexander's siege engines were in place (but before they began firing) a large stretch of wall collapsed because of this sapping. At this collapse, Alexander signalled a general assault around the whole circuit of the city. Areas were the walls had collapsed were stormed, and scaling ladders were used at other points, causing what remained of the defenders to spread themselves out, reducing the numbers able to defend the breach. Once a breach had been made the fate of the city was sealed, and it fell to the Macedonians shortly afterwards. Arrian tells us that up to 17,000 Indians were killed and over 70,000 captured, as well as 500 cavalry and 300 war chariots. It hardly needs to be said that these numbers seem exaggerated, but whatever the real figures, the siege had been bloody and the defenders suffered badly. Alexander lost 100 men with over 1,200 wounded.

After the capture of Sangala, Alexander marched ever further into India. The Hydaspes had been fought probably in May, and the further campaigning had taken another month. Much of this time had been spent in monsoon rains and floods in an unknown land with no end in sight. It is no surprise at all that the army had finally had enough, and refused to go any further. The revolt was not the end of the campaign, however, as Alexander decided to take a circuitous route back to Babylon rather than travel through friendly (already conquered, that is) territory. His intention was to continue to expand the Empire in the process.

The City of the Mallians

Immediately after the revolt on the Hyphasis River, where Alexander agreed to march no further east, the army marched back to the Hydaspes and an enormous fleet was quickly constructed (not far short of 2,000 vessels!) to transport some of the army down river. The remainder marched on land along the banks on either side of the river. After three days sail, the fleet reached a prearranged point where Hephaestion and Craterus, the respective commanders on each bank, had been ordered to halt their advance, and the fleet did likewise. The host paused at this point for two days to gather provisions and await the arrival of Philip, who had evidently been campaigning elsewhere. A couple of days further down the river, news reached Alexander that the Mallians and Oxydracae were preparing resistance to his passage. These were the most warlike of the Indian tribes of the region, and Curtius tells us they could put more than 100,000 men in the field. However exaggerated these figures are we can safely assume they these two tribes represented a formidable opponent for Alexander.[240] Alexander, as always, was simply incapable of resisting the challenge that these tribes presented, and he hastened into their territory with the intention of catching them while they were still making preparations for his advance, although his informant had told him that they had already secured their women and children in their strongest fortresses.

Alexander divided the army, as had by now become very familiar. Nearchus sailed south with the fleet to the borders of Malli territory. Craterus and Philip led a large column down the west bank of the river whilst Hephaestion and Ptolemy were to take separate columns down the east bank three days apart. The main striking column was, of course, led by Alexander himself: the hypaspists, Peitho's *taxis*, half of the Companion Cavalry and Alexander's new favourite unit, the Dahae horse archers.[241] The small lightly armed fast moving columns that Alexander created during and after the Indian campaign were significantly different from those previous to it. The Agrianians and archers had been a standard addition to any flying column; both are here ignored in favour of the Dahae horse archers. Alexander seems to be utterly enamoured of these new troops. They had more flexibility and firepower than the Cretan archers, and proved far more operationally useful to Alexander.

The location of the city of the Malli is unknown, partly because of the changing course of the various rivers that feed the Indus in the region over the centuries. It seems likely, however, that their territory lay either side of the Hydraotes River, and some distance from the confluence of the Ascines River, generally to the northeast of the modern city of Multan.

This flying column marched directly towards the capital city of the Malli, across the Sandar-Bar desert, taking the Mallians utterly by surprise from the north. The campaign against the Malli on the Hydroates was brutal and, by this time, very predictable.[242] Civilians in the area that were caught in the open were slaughtered without mercy. This was a terror campaign like that conducted in Sogdiana a couple of years previously. It is difficult to see what Alexander hoped to achieve by these tactics, other than repression of the populace by a campaign of fear (which may have been goal enough for him).

The first fortified position that Alexander encountered in the region chose resistance. Perhaps as a direct result of Alexander's terror campaign, they feared what would happen to them if they surrendered. After all, how much worse could their fate be if they resisted and failed? Alexander approached the unnamed position and immediately surrounded it with his infantry. The defenders could, apparently, see that sapping operations had begun against the walls. We can presume that there was an unmentioned delay where Alexander probably ordered the construction of a stockade, as at Sangala previously. This delay would have allowed the sapping operations to get underway, as much preparation was no doubt required in the early stages of these engineering activities.

The infantry were close enough for the walls to be peppered with missile fire, perhaps also from smaller artillery pieces that had been brought along for the purpose. This, coupled with the evident sapping operations, persuaded the defenders to abandon the outer walls and fall back to the inner stronghold of the fortification. The Indians continued to resist vigorously, and with some measure of success. On one occasion a small party of Macedonians broke into the inner fortress, and they were fallen upon by the defenders, twenty-five being killed before the remainder managed to escape.

The initial attempt on the inner fortress had met with only limited success, so Alexander ordered full-scale sapping operations to begin, and scaling ladders to be used as the assault continued unabated. We have no clue in the sources as to how long it took the sapping to be effective, but before long a tower was brought down along with a section of the walls, exposing the interior of the fortress. There is a hint in Arrian of the lack of motivation felt by the rank and file that would soon almost cost Alexander his life. Arrian tells us.[243]

> Alexander, ahead of his men, was up (on the collapsed section of wall) in a moment, and stood there alone, a conspicuous figure, holding the breach. The sight of him struck shame into his troops, so up they went after him in scattered groups.

Once the men were shamed into attacking, Alexander quickly captured the city. Some of the Indians, not wishing Alexander to take their possessions, set fire to their houses, and many were caught and killed. In all, around 5,000 Indians died, and only a handful were taken alive. We have no reports of women and children in the city. Perhaps they had been previously evacuated to a stronger position.

Upon the fall of this fortress, Alexander rested his troops for a day, probably also to try and restore some of the evidently flagging morale, before advancing against the remaining Malli cities. Alexander found that the closest Mallian towns were deserted and that the populations had fled into uninhabited regions. There seemed little point in following them, and so, after another day's rest, he continued along the river in the direction of the principle Mallian city (after sending word back to the fleet to send forward the light infantry to join him). Much to Alexander's great disappointment, he found the capital city also deserted with the inhabitants having withdrawn across the Hydroates River. Upon approaching the river, however, he found them massed on the opposite bank showing every sign of opposing his crossing.

The light infantry that Alexander had requested had not yet arrived, and he was only in command of cavalry. Yet, without even pausing for breath, he charged straight into the river to engage the enemy. As soon as the Indians saw Alexander's headlong charge into the river they began to withdraw with the intention of moving to safer ground. Once they realized that Alexander commanded no infantry at all, and that the river was seriously disrupting his charge, they began to reform with the intention of opposing his crossing. Their force was substantial and numbered some 50,000, according to Arrian; Alexander commanded a mere few thousand cavalry. This is an excellent example of Alexander's arrogance getting the better of him. He was attacking at a serious disadvantage in terms of both numbers and troop types (having no infantry at all). He also had charged straight into the river without even allowing his cavalry units time to reform after their rapid advance from the Malli capital. He did manage to regain his composure before what would have been an almost inevitable disaster, however, and kept the cavalry manoeuvring just out of range of the enemy archers. It could have been that he was simply seeing if the Indians would flee at the sight of his cavalry charge, instead of this being an actual attempt at combat. The light-armed infantry, specifically the Agrianians and archers, quickly caught up to the cavalry at the river, and the heavy infantry appeared in the distance; this was enough to force the Mallians to retire to the relative protection of a nearby city, which was heavily fortified, Alexander quick on their heels, to await the inevitable siege.[244]

As soon as Alexander's cavalry arrived at the city, they were ordered to surround the fortifications and ensure nobody gained access, or were able to leave. When the infantry came up at a slightly slower pace, they replaced the cavalry and completely surrounded the walls. A temporary, and presumably rather small, stockade was erected and Alexander then ordered the men to stand firm in their positions. Arrian tells us that there were two reasons that the siege operations did not begin immediately: lack of remaining daylight and that the troops were rather tired from their long march and the crossing of the river.

The following morning, once the infantry were in place and rested, the assault began. Scaling ladders were used and we can presume sapping operations also, given that they had occurred in every recent siege operation with great success. As the Mallians had done during the previous siege, they abandoned the outer ring of defences quickly and retired to the inner fortifications; these Alexander invested without delay. Alexander, at the head of an infantry unit, wrenched a gate from its hinges and penetrated into the town far in advance of Perdiccas and his infantry *taxis*, which was encountering greater resistance than Alexander had done. Once they had breached the outer walls, they saw that the inner fortress was heavily defended, and both Alexander and Perdiccas sent for scaling ladders and ordered sapping operations to begin against these inner walls, again exactly on the same format of the previous siege. The men had not bothered to carry scaling ladders, probably because of a certain lack of enthusiasm to climb up them in the face of concerted opposition. Here we see again the flagging enthusiasm of the infantry that we also saw a week or so earlier at the previous Malli stronghold. They had expected to be travelling home after their mutiny, and Alexander's response to it, but it was evident to them now that Alexander was continuing to campaign just as he had done previously. What makes this reluctance to continue fighting more surprising is that it was largely from the hypaspists, the elite of the heavy infantry, those who were always relied upon to conduct the most difficult operations (such as the naval assault on Tyre). Arrian tells us that:[245]

> The men with the scaling ladders were not quick enough to satisfy
> Alexander; in his impatience he snatched one from the fellow who carried
> it and with his own hands reared it against the fortress wall; then,
> crouched under his shield, up he went.

Alexander was accompanied by only his shield bearer, Peucestas (with the shield of Achilles looted from his tomb at Troy), Leonnatus, an officer, and Abreas, a hand-picked soldier. Only these four had climbed the ladder onto the wall of the inner defences.

Alexander fought wildly and forced back the defenders from his area of the battlements; many Indians lay dead at his feet. He was so successful that the Malli did not dare to approach him, and the four stood alone on top of the battlements in full view of both attackers and defenders. Alexander realized the danger of his very exposed position. He could be picked off by an archer at any moment, and the infantry outside were still showing little enthusiasm to join him atop the battlements. He then leapt down into the inner fortress with only his three colleagues around him. He was now completely surrounded by Indians and in a very dire position indeed.

> Once inside the fortress, he put his back to the wall and made ready to
> fight. A party of Indians came at him, and he cut them down; their
> commander rushed forward, all too rashly, and he, too, fell. First one, then
> a second, who tried to approach him he stopped with a well aimed stone.
> Others pressed within striking distance, and fell victims to his sword.
> After that none ventured again to attack him hand-to-hand; keeping their

distance, they formed a half-circle round where he stood and hurled at him whatever missiles they had or could find.

Abreas was shot in the face and killed, and Alexander too was injured by an arrow that penetrated his corslet and entered his chest, piercing a lung. Alexander soon collapsed from blood loss; Peucestas continued to fight standing astride the fallen king and holding forth the shield of Achilles. Leonnatus stood back to back with Peucestas and both fought desperately to protect their fallen king.[246]

The remainder of the Macedonian army on the outside of the inner wall were so dismayed for the safety of their king, and so ashamed at their own lack of courage, that they immediately grabbed hold of as many ladders as they could and began scaling the walls in their droves. Scaling ladders in the ancient world were a rather rickety affair, and too many men attempted to climb them simultaneously; this caused most to simply collapse under the weight.

The hypaspists, by now, were frantic and tried every means of getting over the walls. Some drove stakes into the clay of the walls and dragged themselves up, others stood on the shoulders of their colleagues (indicating, along with Alexander's leap into the city from the walls, that they were not precipitously high). As soon as any man gained the walls, they leapt into the city in order to protect their prone and unconscious king. A fierce battle ensued with successive Macedonians holding their shields over Alexander. Many died on both sides in these few desperate minutes. Quickly, although it must have seemed like hours, the hypaspists still outside of the walls managed to force open the main gate, and they began to pour into the inner fortress to come to the aid of Alexander; the carnage all around was terrible. Once the main gates were open, the defenders had no chance and the real butchery began: every living soul in the city was slaughtered in a massive act of revenge.[247] Alexander's actions at the city have subsequently become almost legend, but they hide a number of key issues. The army was clearly losing all enthusiasm for continued conquest, and it was only by increasingly-rash acts that Alexander was able to keep them motivated.

The siege of the city of the Mallians was to be Alexander's last major campaign, and it was one that almost cost him his life. From this point, until his death the following year, the campaigns were minor affairs, and not conducted personally by Alexander, given his grave injury. As his final military act, the siege shows at once his bravery and recklessness. Alexander always led from the front. He was always the first to engage the enemy; be that as commander of the Companion Cavalry or the first over a wall during a siege operation. These were characteristics that have given him an enduring legacy but could so easily have cost him his life much earlier, perhaps at the Granicus during the famous incident where he was almost beheaded. We also see in this siege (and also earlier at Sangala) that the Macedonians were utterly tired of constant conflict. They had been promised a journey home, and they could only see endless warfare in front of them. Alexander, had he lived, would soon have had to increasingly rely on native Persian troops such as the 30,000 'Successors', as well as Persian cavalry that he was using more and more. We can only imagine how his tactics would have changed to accommodate the changing structure of the army.

Following the disastrous and infamous march through the Gedrosian Desert, Alexander headed for Susa. There he summoned a number of satraps and troops that were ultimately executed for some quite heinous crimes; Alexander was attempting to restore order and discipline, and at the same time sending a message that he was still in charge. From Susa, the army was divided into several columns, all of which ultimately headed for Babylon where he died in 323.

Alexander the Great was a commander who had mastered the art of adapting a relatively small series of successful tactics to any new situation that he encountered. The tactic of attacking the enemy in more than one direction simultaneously, for example, was, we might imagine, more suited to set-piece battles like Issus or Gaugamela, but repeatedly in sieges he used this tactic in a truly masterful way. At Tyre he attacked from the mole and from aboard ship, and at Gaza he attacked every part of the defences to spread the defenders out as thinly as possible. During set-piece battles Alexander always tried to fight on terrain of his choosing by luring the enemy out of their prepared positions; during siege warfare he frequently tried the same by luring the defenders out.

Throughout his career Alexander demonstrated repeatedly that he was the ancient world's most innovative and adaptable commander, and this is particularly demonstrated during his career as a besieger. The constant innovation and reaction at Tyre is fascinating to read, particularly given that Alexander was on the back foot for much of the time but eventually developed (or adapted) a winning tactic by acquiring a new fleet.

Alexander's set-piece battles are fascinating and will be examined in the succeeding volume, but his sieges arguably give us a better opportunity to examine his tactics closely and his ability to adapt and improvise not just at the outset of a military encounter, but constantly as prevailing circumstance developed.

Alexander advanced the art of siegecraft further and faster than any previous commander had done. No citadel or fortress, no matter how well defended by man or nature, was capable of standing against him: this aspect of his career is worthy of careful study for that very fact alone.

Notes and References

1 Sun Tzu, 1.1–2.
2 Diodorus, 17.87.4.
3 Diodorus, 17.87.5.
4 Arrian, 1, preface.
5 Arrian, 1, preface.
6 Errington, 1969, 237.
7 Arrian, 1.21.2–4; Diodorus, 17.25.5-6.
8 Arrian, 2.21.3.
9 Bosworth, 1980, 245.
10 Curtius, 3.3.1.
11 Curtius, 3.2.10–19; Diodorus 17.30.
12 Curtius, 8.13.13–17– 8.14.19.
13 Curtius, 4.6.29.
14 Curtius, 4.3.11.
15 Curtius, 9.5.21.
16 Curtius, 4.15.18–22. *cf*. 4.12.4; 4.15.12. *cf*. Atkinson, 1980, 61; 400-401; 413; 440–441.
17 Plutarch, *Alex*. 60.1; 60.11.
18 The others being 1.18.6–9 at Miletus; 2.25.2–3 at the Euphrates; 3.10.1–2 at Gaugamela and 3.18.12; at Persepolis.
19 English, 2009, ch.7; *cf*. Rihll, 2007, 27*ff*.
20 Diodorus, 14.41.6.
21 Diodorus, 14.41.3–42.1.
22 Rihll, 2007, 37.
23 Diodorus, 16.74.4; 75.3; Arrian 1.22.2.
24 Rihll, 2007, 78.
25 Ammianus Marcellinus, 24.4.1*ff*. The preceding material is Rihll, 2007, 63–77.

26 Lane Fox, 1973, 137.
27 Arrian, 1.6.1*f.*
28 Arrian, 4.4.
29 Diodorus, 14.50–51
30 Diodorus, 14.51.1.
31 Campbell, 2003, 6; Marsden, 1971, 85.
32 Campbell, 2003, 12.
33 Procopius, *De Bello Gothico* 1.22.
34 Arrian, 1.22.6*f*; 2.19.1-6.
35 Diodorus, 17.26.
36 Arrian, 2.27.3.
37 Arrian, 2.21.7; Diodorus, 17.43.3; Curtius, 4.3.14*ff*; Marsden, 1969, 101,103; Bosworth, 1980, 246.
38 Arrian, 1.1.4; Diodorus, 17.3.5; Ashley, 1998, 166.
39 Justin, 11.6.4.
40 These early campaigns are only recorded in any depth by Arrian, 1.1.4-1.9.8; (the Illyrian campaign to the fall of Thebes).
41 Curtius, 3.10.9.
42 Arrian, 1.5.1; he did so successfully, 1.5.3.
43 Arrian, 1.5.3-5; Livy 31.39.3-6; Bosworth, 1980, 68
44 Arrian, 1.5.5.
45 Ashley, 1998, 171.
46 Arrian, 1.5.8.
47 Hammond, 1974, 80; *contra* Bosworth, 1980, 70.
48 Arrian, 1.6.2.
49 Arrian, 1.6.5; this passage is one of the few that depict the Companion Cavalry as using shields; in all likelihood they did not use them frequently, only when there was an expectation of fighting on foot, see Bosworth, 1980, 72.
50 Arrian, 1.6.9*ff.*
51 Arrian, 1.6.9-11.
52 Arrian, 1.7.1-1.8.6; Diodorus, 17.8-14.
53 Arrian, 1.7.1.
54 Justin, 9.4.7-8.
55 Bosworth, 1980, 74.
56 Bosworth, 1988, 32.
57 Diodorus, 17.8.4-5.
58 Arrian, 1.10.1.

59 Bosworth, 1988, 194.

60 Diodorus, 17.11.2.

61 Arrian, 1.7.7; Diodorus, 17.9.4; has a similar pause before hostilities began, as does Plutarch, *Alex*. 11.

62 Arrian, 1.7.8.

63 Arrian, 1.7.10–11.

64 Given that Ptolemy is explicitly named as the source a few lines later at Arrian 1.8.1., Bosworth, 1980, 80, is in no doubt that this whole section is taken from Ptolemy.

65 Plutarch, *Alex*. 11.

66 Diodorus, 17.11.3–12.

67 Arrian, 1.8.1–8.

68 Diodorus, 17.4. Green,1991, 149.

69 Errington, 1969, 237; *cf*. Roisman, 1984, 376–80.

70 Arrian, 1.18.7.

71 Arrian, 1.19.1.

72 Arrian, 1.19.4.

73 Arrian, 1.20.1. The following section relies heavily on Bosworth, 1980, 141*ff*.

74 Diodorus, 17.22.5, the other being that he believed his troops would fight all the harder if deprived of any means of escape.

75 Curtius, 3.1.19–20.

76 Diodorus, 17.22.5. Green, 1991, 157, notes that all Alexander ever got from Athens were these 20 vessels along with 200 cavalry.

77 Atkinson, 1980, 92, notes a few ships mentioned by Curtius as being stationed at the Hellespont.

78 Hornblower, 1982, 297–305; Hammond, 1988, 47.

77 Arrian, 2.20.2.

80 Arrian, 1.20.4. Diodorus makes no mention of the aborted attack on Myndus.

81 Arrian, 1.20.10.

82 Arrian, 1.21.1–4; Diodorus, 17.25.5–6.

83 Arrian, 1.21.1–2.

84 Arrian, 1.21.4

85 Diodorus, 17.25.6; Arrian, 1.21.3. *cf*. Curtius, 5.4.3; Arrian, 3.18.3 for a further example of Alexander recovering his dead. *cf*. Bosworth, 1980, 146; Lane Fox, 1973, 138.

86 Arrian, 1.22.1.

87 Arrian, 1.22.3. *cf.* Bosworth, 1980, 148; Marsden, 1969, 101-3.

88 Arrian, 1.23.4.

89 Ashley, 1998, 210.

90 For the siege of Tyre see Arrian, 2.16.1-24; Plutarch, *Alex.*, 24-5; Diodorus, 17.40.2-46.6; Justin, 11.10.10-14, *cf.* Polyaenus, 4.3.3-4; 4.13.1.

91 Curtius, 4.2.2.

92 Arrian, 2.15.7. *cf.* Bosworth, 1980, 235.

93 Arrian, 2.16.6; Curtius, 4.2.5.

94 Bosworth, 1988, 65.

95 Arrian, 2.17.1-2.

96 Arrian, 2.18.3; Curtius, 4.2.9.

97 For Harpagones see: Pliny, *NH* 7.56.209; *cf.* Diodorus, 13.50.5. Their use by Alcibiades: Polyaenus, 1.40.9; *cf.* Diodorus, 13.50.5. For ravens see: Polyaenus, 1.22.4*ff*; Curtius, 4.3.26; Appian, BC 5.106. Atkinson, 1980, 297.

98 Polyaenus, 4.3.3.

99 Curtius, 4.2.18; *cf.* Bosworth, 1980, 240

100 Arrian, 2.18.3.

101 Artillery pieces were placed in the towers, Arrian, 3.18.3.

102 Arrian, 2.18.3.

103 For the siege of Motya, see Diodorus, 4.2.23.

104 Bosworth, 1980, 240.

105 Diodorus, 17.42.7; although this is assumed by Fuller, 1958, 210.

106 Curtius, 4.2.8; 3.6-7; Diodorus, 42.5.

107 Curtius, 4.3.6-7.

108 Arrian, 2.19.1.

109 Bosworth, 1980, 240; Morrison & Williams, 1968, 248*f.*

110 Arrian, 2.19.2-3.

111 Curtius, 4.3.2.

112 Arrian, 2.19.4-5.

113 Arrian, 2.19.6.

114 Curtius, 4.2.24.

115 Arrian only twice makes reference to the famous siege engineers, here and at 2.21.1. None of our extant sources mention any of them by name, but we can probably assume that the Thessalian Diades was among them; once famously described as 'the man who took Tyre with Alexander' (Bosworth, 1980, 241). Charias was probably among

them too, the pupil of Polyeidus, Philip's engineer at Perinthus and Byzantium. Charias was no doubt responsible for the stone-throwing catapults used against Halicarnassus, Tyre and later Gaza: Diodorus, 42.7; *cf.* Arrian, 2.21.7; Marsden, 1971, 102*f.*

116 Arrian, 2.20.1-5.
117 Ashley, 1998, 242.
118 Curtius, 4.3.11.
119 Arrian, 2.20.1-3; Plutarch, *Alex* 24.5; Curtius, 4.3.11.
120 Arrian, 2.20.4.
121 Morrison, 2001, 41.
122 Curtius, 4.2.24-3.7.
123 Rutz, 1965, 376*f.*
124 Arrian, 2.20.6.
125 Ashley, 1998, 242.
126 Arrian, 1.21.1.
127 Arrian, 2.21.7; Diodorus, 17.43.3; Curtius, 4.3.14*ff*; Marsden, 1969, 101,103; Bosworth, 1980, 246.
128 Arrian, 2.21.2-3.
129 Diodorus, 17.43.1-2; Curtius, 4.3.24-5; Bosworth, 1980, 247.
130 Arrian, 2.21.5*f.*
131 Arrian, 2.21.7.
132 Arrian, 2.21.4.
133 Bosworth, 1980, 249; Ashley, 1998, 243. For earlier instances of the use of the same strategy see Thucydides, 7.39*f*; Xenophon, *Hellenica*, 2.1.24; Herodotus, 6.78.
134 Fuller, 1958, 214; Bosworth, 1980, 249.
135 Devine, 1988, 3-20 first used the term for the sacrifice of Socrates cavalry at the Granicus in 334.
136 Arrian, 2.21.9; Curtius, 4.4.6-9.
137 Arrian, 2.21.9.
138 Arrian, 2.22.1*f.*
139 Diodorus, 17.43.5-6.
140 Arrian, 2.22.6-7.
141 Diodorus, 17.45.2-3.
142 Diodorus, 17.43.5-6.
143 Diodorus, 17.45.7 for the offer of surrender. Romane, 1987, 85. for the two day delay. Arrian, 2.23.1; Curtius, 4.4.10.
144 Curtius, 4.4.1.

145 Atkinson, 1980, 308.
146 Arrian, 2.23.2*f.*
147 Bosworth, 1980, 253.
148 Diodorus, 17.43.4.
149 For the last stand, see Curtius, 4.2.15; Arrian, 2.24.4. For casualty figures, see Arrian, 2.24.5; Diodorus, 17.46.4, gives the number of captives at 13,000 and claims 2,000 were crucified. Curtius, 4.4.15 adds 15,000 were smuggled to out to Sidon; highly unlikely but these figures also total 30,000.
150 Diodorus, 17.49.1.
151 Arrian, 2.25.1-3; Plutarch, *Alex.* 29.7-8; Diodorus, 17.54.1-5; Curtius, 4.11.1-22. For a full discussion of the chronology and its difficulties see Bosworth, 1980, 256-7. Arrian is almost certainly confusing the peace offer with Alexander's second visit to Tyre; the details of the offer are worthy of note, however.
152 Arrian, 2.25.2-3; the following three quotes are all from this section of Arrian.
153 For details on the visit see Arrian, 3.3.1*ff*; Diodorus, 17.49-51; Curtius 4.7.5-30; Plutarch, *Alex.* 26-27 and Strabo, 17.1.43. For Siwah see Curnow, 2004, 33*f.*
154 Engels, 1978, particularly 54-70; 113-131; 144-158.
155 Bosworth, 1980, 257-258; Atkinson, 1980, 334-336; Romane, 1988, 23.
156 Curtius, 4.6.7; Arrian, 2.25.4; Josephus, *AJ.* 11.320.
157 Bosworth, 1980, 258; Diodorus, 16.47.4; *cf.* 16.50.8.
158 For Arab Mercenaries at Gaza see Arrian, 2.25.4. For Raphia see Polybius, 5.79.8, 82.12; *cf.* Bosworth, 1980, 258. For Batis preparations see Arrian, 2.25.4. For the motivation of defenders see Curtius, 4.6.7.
159 Bosworth, 1980, 258.
160 Curtius, 4.6.8; Arrian, 2.26.2.
161 Arrian, 2.26.2.
162 Arrian, 2.26.2.
163 Curtius, 4.6.8-9; Arrian, 2.26.2-3.
164 Ashley, 1998, 249, fn.177, following Bosworth, 1980, 258.
165 Plutarch *Alex.* , 25.4; Arrian, 2.16.2-3; Curtius, 4.6.11. For information on torsion and non-torsion catapults see Marsden, 1971.
166 Curtius, 4.6.11.

167 Thucydides, 2.77.

168 Thucydides, 4.100

169 Arrian, 2.27.1; *cf.* Bosworth, 1980, 259.

170 Arrian, 2.27.1.

171 Curtius, 4.6.15-16.

172 Curtius, 4.6.

173 Arrian, 2.27.3; Curtius, 4.6.21.

174 Fuller, 1958, 217, supported by Bosworth, 1980, 259.

175 Arrian, 2.27.3.

176 Arrian, 2.27.4.

177 Arrian, 2.27.4-6.

178 Curtius, 4.6.29.

179 Green, 1974, 541 n.58, citing Sophocles, *Ajax*, 1029-1031 & Euripides, *Andromache*, 339; *cf.* Atkinson, 1980, 342.

180 Arrian, 2.27.7.

181 Diodorus, 17.68.1; Curtius, 5.3.17; Arrian, 3.18.2.

182 Diodorus, 17.68.2-3; Curtius, 5.3.17-23; Arrian, 3.18.3.

183 Curtius, 5.4.20; Arrian, 3.18.6.

184 Arrian, 3.18.6; Strabo, 729; Curtius, 5.5.2-4; Diodorus, 17.69.2. *cf.* Bosworth, 1980, 327.

185 Bosworth, 1988, 91.

186 Curtius, 5.4.33.

187 Curtius, 7.11.1*ff*; Bosworth, 1981, 36; Bosworth, 1988, 113; *contra* Ashley, 1998, 301; places the siege in the spring of 327 following Arrian.

188 Curtius, 7.11.1*ff.*

189 Arrian, 4.19.1; Curtius, 7.11.7.

190 Curtius, 7.11.10-11.

191 Arrian, 4.19.1.

192 Curtius, 7.11.13.

193 Curtius, 7.11.16.

194 Curtius, 7.11.28; *Metz Epitome* 18; Arrian, 4.19.4-5, *cf.* 4.16.3.

195 Arrian, 4.19.2; Curtius, 7.11.19.

196 Arrian, 4.18.1; Curtius, 8.2.19; reads Nauta; *Metz Epitome*, 19; reads Nautace.

197 Arrian, 4.21.2.

198 Arrian, 4.21.4-5; Curtius, 8.2.23-4; *cf.* Bosworth, 1988, 117; Bosworth, 1995, 136-7.

199 Curtius, 8.2.26.
200 Arrian, 4.21.6.
201 Arrian, 7.6.1; Plutarch, *Alex.* 71.1; Diodorus, 17.108.1-3; Curtius, 7.5.1.
202 Arrian, 4.15.6.
203 English, 2009.
204 Bosworth, 1988, 119.
205 Arrian, 4.22.7.
206 Heckel, 2008, 116.
207 Bosworth, 1988, 121.
208 Arrian, 4.23.4-5; Curtius, 8.10.6.
209 Arrian, 4.24.7; *cf.* Bosworth, 1988, 121.
210 Arrian, 4.26.1; Curtius, 8.10.23, puts the Massaga garrison at 38,000 infantry; *cf.* Ashley, 1998, 462; Bosworth, 1988, 122.
211 Curtius, 8.10.24.
212 Arrian, 4.26.2.
213 Arrian, 4.26.2*f.*
214 Curtius, 8.10.27.
215 Curtius, 8.10.30; Arrian, 4.26.4.
216 Curtius, 8.10.32.
217 Arrian, 4.27.6.
218 Arrian, 4.27.3, Diodorus, 17.84.1-2; *cf.* Plutarch, *Alex.*, 59.3-4.
219 Curtius, 8.10.34-35.
220 Arrian, 4 27.5; Stein, 1929, 53-61.
221 Arrian, 4.27.5.
222 Who calls the town Ecbolima.
223 For Embolina/Ecbolima see: Arrian, 4.28.7; Curtius, 8.12.1. For Pir-Sar see: Arrian, 4.28.1; Stein, 1929, 128*ff. contra* Tucci, 1977, 52-5; Eggermont, 1984 and (tentatively) Badian, 1987, 117, n.1, all argue for Mt. Ilam instead of Pir-sar. For a re-affirmation of Pir-Sar as the rightful location of the Rock of Aornus, see Bosworth, 1995, 179-80.
224 Diodorus, 17.85.2; *cf.* Curtius, 8.11.2.
225 Arrian, 4.28.7.
226 Bosworth, 1995, 189.
227 Arrian, 4.29.6.
228 Diodorus, 17.85.6; Curtius, 8.11.7-8. *Cf.* Stein, 1929, 118-9; Bosworth, 1995, 189.
229 Arrian, 4.30.1.

230 Curtius, 8.12.1; *cf.* Diodorus, 17.82.2, who calls the man Aphrices.

231 Arrian, 5.20.2.

232 Arrian, 5.22.4–6; Curtius, 9.1.17.

233 Arrian, 5.22.6.

234 Arrian, 5.23.1; Curtius, 9.1.15.

235 Curtius, 9.1.15.

236 Curtius, 9.1.17.

237 Arrian, 5.24.2.

238 Arrian, 5.24.2.

239 Arrian, 5.24.4.

240 Curtius, 90,000 Infantry, 10,000 Cavalry and 900 chariots. Diodorus notes 80,000 infantry, 10,000 cavalry and 700 chariots; Arrian 6.8.5*ff.* notes 50,000 Mallians.

241 Arrian, 6.6.4.

242 It is known only from Arrian, 6.6–10.

243 Arrian, 6.8.2.

244 Arrian, 6.9.1.

245 Arrian, 6.9.3 (as well as quote below); *cf.* Curtius, 9.4.30.

246 Arrian, 6.10.1; Curtius, 9.5.9–10; Diodorus, 17.99.3; Plutarch, *Alex.*, 63.9.

247 Arrian, 6.11.1; Curtius, 9.5.20; Diodorus, 17.99.4.

Bibliography

Anderson, J K, *Military Theory and Practice in the Age of Xenophon* (Berkley, 1970)

Anspach, A E, *De Alexandri Magni expeditione Indica* (Leipzig, 1903)

Ashley, J R, *The Macedonian Empire: The Era of Warfare Under Philip II and Alexander the Great* (London, 1998)

Atkinson, J C, *A Commentary on Q. Curtius Rufus' Historiae Alexandri Magni, Books 3 and 4* (Amsterdam, 1980)

Badian, E, 'The Eunuch Bagoas: A Study in Method', *CQ* 8, 1958, 144-57

Badian, E, 'The First Flight of Harpalus', *Historia* 9, 1960, 245-6

Badian, E, 'The Death of Philip II', *Phoenix* 17, 1963, 244-50

Badian,E, 'Orientals in Alexander's Army', *JHS* 85, 1965a, 160-1

Badian, E, 'The Administration of the Empire', *Greece and Rome* 12, 1965b, 166-82

Badian, E, 'The Date of Cleitarchus', *PACA* 1965c, 1-11

Badian, E, 'Alexander the Great and the Greeks of Asia', *Ancient Society and Institutions* (Studies Presented to V. Ehrenburg, Oxford, 1966), 37-69

Badian, E, *Studies in Greek and Roman History* (London, 1968)

Badian, E, 'Some Recent Interpretations of Alexander', *Fondation Hardt Entretiens* 22 (Geneva, 1976)

Badian, E, 'The Battle of the Granicus: A New Look', *Ancient Macedonia* 2 (Thessalokini, 1977), 271-293

Badian, E, 'Alexander at Peucelaotis', *CQ* 37, 1987, 117-28

Badian, E, 'Agis III: Revisions and Reflections', in Worthington, I, (ed.), *Ventures into Greek History* (Oxford, 1994), 258-92

Bauer, A, 'Die Schlacht bei Issos', *Ost. Jb.* 2, 1899, 105-128

Beloch, K J, *Griechische Geschichte* (Berlin, 1923)

Berve, H, *Das Alexanderreich auf prosopographischer Grundlage* (Munich, 1926)

Bieber, M, *Alexander the Great in Greek and Roman Art* (Chicago, 1964)

Bigwood, J M, 'Ctesias as Historian', *Phoenix* 32, 1978, 19-41

Billows, R, 'Polybius and Alexander Historiography', in Bosworth, A B, & Baynham, E J, (ed.), *Alexander the Great in Fact and Fiction* (Oxford, 2000)

Bloedow, E F, 'On "Wagons" and "Shields": Alexander's Crossing of Mt. Haemus in 335 BC', *The Ancient History Bulletin* 10.3-4, 1996, 119-130

Bose, P, *Alexander the Great's Art of Strategy* (London, 2003)

Bosworth, A B, 'Philip II and Upper Macedonia', *CQ* 21, 1971, 93-105

Bosworth, A B, 'Arrian and the Alexander Vulgate', *Fondation Hardt Entretiens* 22, 1976, 1-46

Bosworth, A B, *Commentary on Arrian's History of Alexander* vol I (Oxford, 1980)

Bosworth, A B, 'Alexander and the Iranians', *JHS* 100, 1980b, 1-21

Bosworth, A B, 'A Missing Year in the History of Alexander the Great', *JHS* 101, 1981, 17-39

Bosworth, A B, *Conquest and Empire, The Reign of Alexander the Great* (Cambridge, 1988)

Bosworth, A B, *From Arrian to Alexander: Studies in Historical Interpretation* (London, 1988b)

Bosworth, A B, *Commentary on Arrian's History of Alexander* vol II (Oxford, 1995)

Bosworth, A B, & Baynham, E J, (ed.), *Alexander the Great in Fact and Fiction* (Oxford, 2000)

Bosworth, A B, 'Plus ça change... Ancient Historians and their Sources', *Classical Antiquity* 22, 2003, 167-198

Bosworth, A B, 'Introduction: Some Basic Principles', in Worthington, I, *Alexander the Great: A Reader* (London, 2003b)

Brunt, P A, 'Persian Accounts of Alexander's Campaigns', *CQ* 12, 1962, 141-55

Brunt, P A, 'Alexander's Macedonian Cavalry', *JHS* 83, 1963, 27-46

Brunt, P A, *Arrian: History of Alexander and Indica* (Loeb Classical Library) I-II (Cambridge, 1976-83)

Burn, A R, 'Notes on Alexander's Campaigns', 332-330, *JHS* 72, 1952, 81-91

Burn, A R, *Alexander the Great and the Hellenistic World*, (London, 1947)

Burn, A R, 'Notes on Alexander's Campaigns', *JHS* 72, 1952, 81-91

Campbell, D B, *Greek and Roman Siege Machinery* (Oxford, 2003)

Carmen, J, & Harding, A, (eds.), *Ancient Warfare: Archaeological Perspectives* (Stroud, Gloucestershire, 1999)

Canto, N F, *Alexander the Great: Journey to the End of the Earth* (London, 2005)

Caroe, O, *The Pathans* (London, 1962)

Cartledge, P, *Alexander the Great: The Hunt for a New Past* (London, 2004)

Casson, L, *Ships and Seamen in the Ancient World* (Princeton, 1971)

Cawthorne, N, *Alexander the Great* (London, 2004)

Clark, M, 'Did Thucydides Invent the Battle Exhortation?', *Historia* 44, 1995, 375-6

Cook, J M, *The Persian Empire* (New York, 1983)

Dahmen, K, *The Legend of Alexander the Great on Greek and Roman Coins* (London, 2007)

Davis, E W, 'The Persian Battle Plan at the Granicus', *James Sprunt Studies in History and Political Science* 46, 1964, 34-44

Delbrück, H, *Geschichte der Kriegskunst im Rahmen der Politischen Geschichte* (Berlin 1920), tr. Renfroe, W J, History of the Art of War within the Framework of Political History (London, 1975)

Devine, A M, 'The Location of the Battlefield of Issus', *LCM* 5, 1980, 3-10

Devine, A M, 'A Note on Tactical Terms', *LCM* 7, 1982, 62-63

Devine, 'A M, Embolon: A Study in Tactical Terminology', *Phoenix* 37, 1983, 201-217

Devine, A M, 'The Strategies of Alexander the Great and Darius III in the Issus Campaign', *Ancient World* 12, 1985a, 25-38

Devine, A M, 'Grand Tactics at the Battle of Issus', *Ancient World* 12, 1985b, 39-59

Devine, A M, 'The Battle of Gaugamela', *Ancient World* 13, 1986, 87-116

Devine, A M, 'The Battle of the Hydaspes: A Tactical and Source-Critical Study', *Ancient World* 16, 1987, 91-113

Devine, A M, 'A Pawn-Sacrifice at the Battle of the Granicus', *Ancient World* 18, 1988, 3-20

Dinsmoor, W B, *Archons of Athens* (Cambridge, Mass. 1931)

Dittberner, W, *Issos, ein Beitrag zur Geschichte Alexanders des Großen* (Berlin, 1908)

Dodge, T A, *Alexander the Great Vols I–II* (Boston, 1890)

von Domaszewski, A, 'Die Phalangen Alexanders und Caesars Legionen', *Heidelberger Sitz. – Ber. Phil. – hist. Kl.* 16, 1925, 50-65

Doherty, P, *Alexander the Great: The Death of a God* (London, 2004)

Eadie, J W, 'The Development of Roman Mailed Cavalry', *JRS* 57, 1967, 161-173

Eggermont, P H L, 'Alexander's Campaign in Gandhara and Ptolemy's list of Indo-Scythian Towns', *Orientalia Lovaniensia Periodica* 1, 1970, 63-123

Eggermont, P H L, 'Ptolemy the Geographer and the People of the Dards', *OLP* 15, 1984, 191-200

Ellis, J R, 'Alexander's Hypaspists Again', *Historia* 24, 1975, 617-618

Engels, D W, *Alexander the Great and the Logistics of the Macedonian Army* (California, 1978)

English, S, 'Hoplites or Peltasts: The Macedonian "Heavy" Infantry', *Ancient Warfare* 2.1, 2008, 32-35

English, S, *The Army of Alexander the Great* (Barnsley, 2009)

Erhardt, C T H R, 'Speeches before Battle?', *Historia* 44, 1995, 120-1

Errington, R M, 'Bias in Ptolemy's History of Alexander', *CQ* 19 (1969), 233-242

Errington, R, M, *A History of Macedonia* (California, 1990)

Everson, T, *Warfare in Ancient Greece* (Stroud, Gloucestershire, 2004)

Farrokh, K, *Shadows in the Desert: Ancient Persia at War* (Oxford, 2007)

Foss, C, 'The Battle of the Granicus River: A New Look', *Ancient Macedonia 2* (Thessalokini, 1977), 495-502

Fraser, P M, *Cities of Alexander the Great* (Oxford, 1996)

Fuller, J F C, *The Generalship of Alexander the Great* (London, 1958)

Green, P, *Alexander of Macedon, 356-323 BC* (Oxford, 1974)

Green, P, *Alexander the Great and the Hellenistic Age* (London, 2007)

Griffith, G T, *The Mercenaries of the Hellenistic World* (Cambridge, 1935)

Griffith, G T, 'Alexander's Generalship at Gaugamela', *JHS* 67, 1947, 77-89

Griffith, G T, 'A Note on the Hipparchies of Alexander', *JHS* 83, 1963, 68-75

Griffith, G T, 'Peltasts and the Origins of the Macedonian Phalanx', in Dell, H J, (ed.), *Ancient Macedonian Studies in Honour of Charles F Edson* (Thessalonika, 1981)

Guderian, H, *Achtung-Panzer!* (Munich 1937), Duffy, C, (tr.) *Achtung-Panzer!* (London, 1995)

Hackett, J, (ed.), *Warfare in the Ancient World* (London, 1989)

Hamilton, J R, 'Three Passages in Arrian', *CQ* 5, 1955, 217-21

Hamilton, J R, 'The Cavalry Battle at the Hydaspes', *JHS* 76, 1956, 26-31

Hamilton, J R, 'The Letters in Plutarch's *Alexander*', *PACA* 4, 1961, 9-20

Hamilton, J R, *Plutarch, Alexander: A Commentary* (London, 1969)

Hamilton, J R, 'Alexander and the Aral', *CQ* 21, 1971, 106-111

Hamilton, J R, *Alexander the Great* (London, 1973)

Hammond, N G L, 'The Macedonian Navies of Philip and Alexander Until 330 BC', *Antichthon* 26, 1992, 30-41

Hammond, N G L, 'Alexander's Campaign in Illyria', *JHS* 94, 1974, 66-87

Hammond, N G L, and Griffith, G T, *A History of Macedonia ii: 550-336 BC* (Oxford, 1979)

Hammond, N G L, 'The Battle of the Granicus River', *JHS* 100, 1980, 73-89

Hammond, N G L, *Alexander the Great: King Commander and Statesman* (London, 1980b)

Hammond, N G L, 'Some Passages in Arrian Concerning Alexander', *CQ* 30, 1980c, 455-76

Hammond, N G L, *Three Historians of Alexander the Great* (Cambridge, 1983)

Hammond, N G L, and Walbank, F W, *History of Macedonia*, vol. 3 (Oxford, 1988)

Hammond, N G L, *Alexander the Great: King, Commander and Statesman* (Bristol, 1989)

Hammond, N G L, *The Macedonian State. The Origins, Institutions and History* (Oxford, 1989b)

Hammond, N G L, 'Some Passages in Polyaenus' Stratagems Concerning Alexander', *GRBS* 37, 1996, 23-54

Hammond, N G L, 'A Papyrus Commentary on Alexander's Balkan Campaign', *GRBS* 28, 1997, 332-348

Hammond, N G L, *The Genius of Alexander the Great* (London, 1997)

Hammond, N G L, 'Cavalry Recruited in Macedonian Down to 322 BC', *Historia* 47, 1998, 404-425

Hansman, J, 'Elamites, Achaemenians and Anshan', *Iran* 10, 1972, 101-25

Hansen, M H, 'The Battle Exhortation in Ancient Historiography', *Historia* 42, 1993, 161-80

Hanson, V D, *The Western Way of War: Infantry Battle in Classical Greece* (New York, 1989)

Harl, K W, 'Alexander's Cavalry Battle at the Granicus', *Polis and Polemos* (Claremont, 1997), 303-326

Hasluck, F W, *Cyzicus* (Cambridge, 1910)

Hauben, H, 'The Command Structure of Alexander's Mediterranean Fleets', *Ancient Society* 3, 1972, 56

Heckel, W, *The Marshals of Alexander's Empire* (London, 1992)

Heckel, W, *The Wars of Alexander the Great: 336-323 BC* (Oxford, 2002)

Heckel, W, de Souza, P, Llewellyn-Jones, L, *The Greeks at War: From Athens to Alexander* (Oxford, 2004)

Heckel, H, *The Conquests of Alexander the Great* (Cambridge, 2008)

Hogarth, D G, *Philip and Alexander of Macedon* (London, 1897)

Holt, Alexander's Settlements in Central Asia, *Ancient Macedonia* 4, 1986, 315-323

Holt, F L, *Alexander the Great and Bactria* (Leiden, The Netherlands, 1989)

Holt, F L, *Into the Land of Bones: Alexander the Great in Afghanistan* (London, 2005)

Janke, A, *Auf Alexanders des Grossen Pfaden. Eine Reise durch Kleinasein* (Berlin, 1904)

Janke, A, 'Die Schlacht bei Issus', *Klio* 10, 1910, 137-177

Judeich, A, 'Die Schlacht am Granikos', *Klio* 8, 1908, 372-97

Judeich, W, in Kromayer, J, and Veith, G, (eds.), *Antike Schlachtfelder IV* (Berlin, 1929)

Kaerst, J, *Geschichte des Hellenismus* (Leipzig, 1927)

Keegan, J, *The Mask of Command* (New York, 1987)

Keipert, H, 'Das Schlachtfeld am Granikos', *Globus* 32, 1887, 263ff

Kedar, B Z, *The Horns of Hattin* (London, 1992)

Kern, P B, *Ancient Siege Warfare* (London, 1999)

Kornemann, E, *Die Alexandergeschichte des Konigs von Aegypten* (Berlin, 1935)

Krensky, S, *Conqueror and Hero: The Search for Alexander* (Boston, 1981)

Lamb, H, *Alexander the Great: The Journey to World's End* (London 1946)

Landels, J G, 'Ship-Shape and *Sambuca*-Fashion', *JHS* 86, 1966, 69-77

Lane Fox, R, *Alexander the Great* (London, 1973)

Leaf, W, *Strabo on the Troad* (Cambridge, 1923)

Lendon, J E, *Soldiers & Ghosts: A History of Battle in Classical Antiquity* (New York, 2005)

Lloyd, A B, (ed.), *Battle in Antiquity* (London, 1996)

Lonsdale, *Alexander: Killer of Men* (London, 2004)

Lonsdale, D J, *Alexander the Great: Lessons in Strategy* (London, 2007)

Lorimer, H L, 'The Hoplite Phalanx', *BSA* 42, 1947, 76-138

Manti, P A, 'The Cavalry Sarissa', *Ancient World* 8, 1983, 73-80

Manti, P A, 'The Sarissa of the Macedonian Infantry', *Ancient World* 23.2, 1992, 31-42

Manti, P A, 'The Macedonian Sarissa, again', *Ancient World* 25.1, 1994, 77-91

Markle, M M, 'The Macedonian Sarissa, Spear, and Related Armour', *AJA* 81, 1977, 323-339

Markle, M M, 'Use of the Macedonian Sarissa by Philip and Alexander', *AJA* 82, 1978, 483-497

Markle, M M, 'Macedonian Arms and Tactics under Alexander the Great', *Studies in The History of Art*, Vol 10 (Washington, 1982), 86-111

Marsden, E W, *The Campaign of Gaugamela* (Liverpool, 1964)

Marsden, E W, *Greek and Roman Artillery: Historical Developments* (Oxford, 1969)

Marsden, E W, *Greek and Roman Artillery: Technical Treatises* (Oxford, 1971)

May, E C, Stadler, G P, & Votan, J F, *Ancient and Medieval Warfare* (Wayne, N.J., 1984)

Mayor, A, *Greek Fire, Poison Arrows & Scorpion Bombs* (New York, 2003)

McKenchie, P, 'Manipulation of themes in Quintus Curtius Rufus Book 10', *Historia* 48, 1999, 44-60

McQueen, E I, 'Quintus Curtius Rufus', in *Latin Biography*; ed. Dorey, T A, (London, 1967) 17-43

Messenger, C, *The Art of Blitzkrieg* (London, 1976)

Milns, R D, 'Alexander's Macedonian Cavalry and Diodorus 17.17.4', *JHS* 86, 1966, 167-168

Milns, R D, 'Philip II and the Hypaspists', *Historia* 16, 1967, 509-12

Milns, R D, *Alexander the Great* (London, 1968)

Milns, R D, 'The Hypaspists of Alexander III: Some Problems', *Historia* 20, 1971, 186-195

Miltner, F, 'Alexander's Strategie bei Issos', *Ost Jh.* 28, 1933, 69-78

Mixter, J R, 'The Length of the Macedonian Sarissa During the Reigns of Philip II and Alexander the Great', *Ancient World* 23.2, 1992, 21-29

Montagu, J D, *Greek & Roman Warfare: Battles Tactics and Trickery* (London, 2006)

Morrison, J S, & R. T Williams, R T, *Greek Oared Ships 900-322 BC* (Cambridge, 1968)

Morrison, A, 'Combat Psychology, and Persepolis', *Antichthon* 35, 2001, 30-44

Mughal, M R, 'Excavations at Tulamba, West Pakistan', *Pakistan Archaeology* 4, 1967, 1-152

Murison, J A, 'Darius III and the Battle of Issus', *Historia* 21, 1972, 399-423

O'Brien, J M, *Alexander the Great: The Invisible Enemy* (London, 1992)

Papazoglu, F, *The Central Balkan Tribes in Pre-Roman Times* (Amsterdam, 1978)

Pearson, L, *The Lost Histories of Alexander the Great* (New York, 1960)

Parke, H W, *Greek Mercenary Soldiers* (Oxford, 1933)

Pritchett, W K, *Essays in Greek History* (Amsterdam, 1994)

Rahe, P A, 'The Annihilation of the Sacred Band at Chaeronea', *AJA* 85, 1981, 84-87

Renfroe, W J, *History of the Art of War within the Framework of Political History* (London, 1975)

Rhodes, P J, & Osborne, R, *Greek Historical Inscriptions, 404-323 BC* (Oxford, 2007)

Rhodes, P J, *A History of the Classical Greek World: 478-323 BC* (Oxford, 2006)

Rice, E E, *Alexander the Great* (Stroud, Gloucestershire, 1997)

Roisman, J, 'Ptolemy and His Rivals in His History of Alexander', *CQ* 34, 1984, 373-385

Romane, P, 'Alexander's Siege of Tyre', *Ancient World* 16, 1987, 79-90

Romane, P, 'Alexander's Siege of Gaza – 332 BC', *Ancient World* 18, 1988, 21-30

Rubin, B, 'Die Entstehung der Kataphraktenreiterei im Lichte der Chorezmischen Ausgrabungen', *Historia* 4, 1955, 264-83

Rutz, W, 'Zur Erzahlungskunst des Q. Curtius Rufus', *Hermes* 93, 1965, 370-82

Sabin, P, van Wees, H, Whitby, M, (eds.), *The Cambridge History of Greek and Roman Warfare* (Cambridge, 2007)

Sage, M M, *Warfare in Ancient Greece* (London, 1996)

Savill, A, *Alexander the Great and His Time* (New York, 1993)

Schachermeyr, F, *Alexander der Grosse* (Vienna, 1973)

Schwartz, E, (ed. Pauley), *Realencyclopadie der Classischen Altertumswissenschaft* (Stuttgart, 1893)

Sekunda, N, *The Army of Alexander the Great* (London, 1984)

Sekunda, N, & Warry, J, *Alexander the Great* (Oxford 2004)

Sekunda, N, 'Land Forces in Sabin', van Wees & Whitby (eds.) *The Cambridge History of Greek and Roman Warfare* (Cambridge, 2007)

Serrati, J, 'Warfare and the State in Sabin', van Wees & Whitby (eds.) *The Cambridge History of Greek and Roman Warfare* (Cambridge, 2007)

Shrimpton, G, 'The Persian Cavalry at Marathon', *Phoenix* 34, 1980, 20-37

Sidnell, P, *Warhorse: Cavalry in Ancient Warfare* (London, 2006)

Smith, V, *The Early History of India* (Oxford, 1914)

Snodgrass, A M, *Arms and Armour of the Greeks* (Ithaca, N.Y., 1967)

Spence, I G, *The Cavalry of Ancient Greece; A social and Military History* (Oxford, 1993)

Stark, F, *Alexander's Path* (London, 1958)

Stein, A, 'The Site of Alexander's Passage of the Hydaspes and the Battle with Porus', *Geographical Journal* 80, 1932, 31-46

Stein, A, *Archaeological Reconnaissance's in North-Western India and South-Eastern Iran* (London, 1937)

Stein, A, 'Notes on Alexander's Crossing of the Tigris and the Battle of Arbela', *Geographical Journal* 100, 1942, 155-164

Strasburger, H, *Ptolemaios und Alexander* (Leipzig, 1934)

Strasburger, H, 'Alexander's Zug Durch die Gedrosische Wüste', *Hermes* 80, 1952, 456-493

Talbert, R J A, (ed.), *Barrington Atlas of Greek and Roman World* (Oxford, 2000)

Tarn, W W, *The Greeks of Bactria and India* (Cambridge, 1938)

Tarn, W W, *Alexander the Great* Vols. I-II (Cambridge, 1948)

Thompson, M, *Granicus 334 BC: Alexander's First Persian Victory* (Oxford, 2007)

Tod, M N, *A Selection of Greek Historical Inscriptions. 2: From 403 to 323 BC* (Oxford, 1948)

Tritle, L A, (ed.), *The Greek World in the Fourth Century* (London, 1997)

Tucci, G, 'On Swat, the Dards and connected problems', *East and West* 27, 1977, 9-103

Veith, G, 'Der Kavalleriekampf in der Schlacht am Hydaspes', *Klio* 8, 1908, 131-53.

van Wees, H, *Greek Warfare: Myths and Realities* (London, 2004)

Wilcken, U, *Alexander the Great* (London, 1932)

Worthington, I, *Alexander the Great: A Reader* (London, 2003)

Worthington, I, *Alexander the Great: Man and God* (London, 2004)

Yalichev, S, *Mercenaries of the Ancient World* (London, 1997)

Index